THE "I LOVE Cookies" RECIPE BOOK

THE "I LOVE Cookies" RECIPE BOOK

From Rolled Sugar Cookies to Snickerdoodles and More,
100 of Your Favorite Cookie Recipes!

JACQUELYN PARKES

ADAMS MEDIA

NEW YORK   LONDON   TORONTO   SYDNEY   NEW DELHI

Adams Media
An Imprint of Simon & Schuster, Inc.
100 Technology Center Drive
Stoughton, Massachusetts 02072

First Adams Media hardcover edition November 2022

ADAMS MEDIA and colophon are trademarks of Simon & Schuster.

For information about special discounts for bulk purchases, please contact Simon & Schuster Special Sales at 1-866-506-1949 or business@simonandschuster.com.

The Simon & Schuster Speakers Bureau can bring authors to your live event. For more information or to book an event contact the Simon & Schuster Speakers Bureau at 1-866-248-3049 or visit our website at www.simonspeakers.com.

Interior design by Erin Alexander
Photographs by Kelly Jaggers

Manufactured in the United States of America

1 2022

Library of Congress Control Number: 2022944541

ISBN 978-1-5072-2004-7
ISBN 978-1-5072-2005-4 (ebook)

Always follow safety and commonsense cooking protocols while using kitchen utensils, operating ovens and stoves, and handling uncooked food. If children are assisting in the preparation of any recipe, they should always be supervised by an adult.

Contains material adapted from the following title published by Adams Media, an Imprint of Simon & Schuster, Inc.: *The Everything® Cookies & Brownies Cookbook* by Marye Audet, copyright © 2009, ISBN 978-1-60550-125-3.

Contents

CHAPTER 6
Slice and Bake Cookies 121

CHAPTER 7
Holiday Favorites 149

Introduction

If you're a cookie lover—and because you have this book in your hands, you must be—you know that fresh-baked cookies are some of the absolutely best things. The way they fill the house with that delicious smell, melt in your mouth while still warm from the oven, and look so cute and cheerful when decorated—it can't help but bring a big smile to your face. And now with *The "I Love Cookies" Recipe Book*, you can bake up a batch of happy any time you want.

This book features one hundred recipes for your favorite cookies. From simple drop cookies, brownies, and bars, to shaped cookies and rolled cookies and convenient slice and bake cookies—this book has it all covered. You'll also find festive cookies to help celebrate the holidays!

These recipes are as easy as they are tasty, and there's something for everyone. Love chocolate? Try the Double Chocolate Chip Cookies, Triple Chocolate Frosted Cookies, or Mudslides. Traditionalists will love the Classic Oatmeal Cookies, Snickerdoodles, Lemon Bars, and Whoopie Pies. The Cinnamon Roll Cookies, Carrot Cake Cookies, Black Forest Cookies, and Eggnog Cookies put your favorite flavors in cookie form! Try something new and deliciously different with Pink Lemonade Cookies, Matcha White Chocolate Chip Cookies, or Lemon and Black Pepper Cookies.

But before you preheat your oven, check out Chapter 1, where you will find the basics of baking cookies including easy-to-learn skills that ensure success, essential ingredients and equipment, beautiful decorating techniques anyone can master, and storage methods that keep your cookies fresh and delicious.

Whether you're looking for a classic like the Peanut Butter Blossoms, a sweet-savory combo like the Chubby Hubby Cookies, or a fruity bite of Blueberry Crumble Bars, you can't go wrong. So turn the page, pick out a recipe, and get ready to taste something delicious. It's time to get this cookie party started. Enjoy!

CHAPTER 1
Cookie Baking Basics

Successful cookie baking is a skill that anyone can learn. This chapter will give you a basic understanding of the ingredients, equipment, and methods of measuring and mixing that are the essential parts of creating the perfect cookie every time. Once the cookies are baked, knowing how to decorate them and store them allows any baker to create professional-looking cookies for any occasion. Before you choose a recipe, read this chapter to ensure your success!

Ingredients for Success

All cookies have the same basic ingredients:

- Flour
- Sugar
- Fat
- Flavoring
- Leavening

It is the variations in these ingredients that produce the differences in the many varieties of cookies. Once you know how the ingredients affect the finished cookie, you can create numerous variations for any recipe and get a predictable result every time. Let's examine each of these ingredients individually.

Flour

There are different types of flour for different types of baking. Most cookie recipes call for all-purpose flour. All-purpose, or white, flour is not as delicate as cake flour and has more protein. This means that it can develop gluten and become tough if mixed for too long. Most recipes will direct you to stir in the flour rather than beating it in so the cookies do not come out tough.

You can substitute whole-wheat flour for part of the all-purpose flour in most recipes if you want. However, too much whole-wheat flour will make your cookies heavy, so beware of a ratio higher than 50/50 wheat to white. If you have an allergy to wheat or gluten, you can substitute a good gluten-free baking mix for the flour in almost any recipe.

Sugar

Sugar is what adds the sweetness to the cookie. It also works with the other ingredients to create the individual texture of each type of cookie. This is why, when you try to substitute a low-calorie sweetener for sugar in a recipe, the texture is often not what you expected. It is usually better to use a recipe written specifically for sugar-free cookies than to try to adapt an old favorite.

White sugar allows the flavor of the cookie to come through, while brown sugar adds a flavor all its own. Honey is sometimes substituted for sugar in recipes, but it will also change the texture of the finished product, and the other liquids in the recipe will need to be decreased. Brown sugar can become rock-hard when improper storage allows the moisture to evaporate. To soften it up, just add a slice or two of fresh bread and seal the bag. The next day, the bread will be extremely stale, but the brown sugar will be soft and easy to work with.

Fat

Fat is what makes a cookie chewy, crumbly, or crisp. Butter is the preferred fat in most cookie recipes because of the delicate flavor it adds. Using all butter can make your cookies very thin, though, so if you consistently seem to have paper-thin cookies when you want thick and chewy ones, try substituting half the butter with a vegetable shortening.

Some very old, heirloom recipes will call for lard. The lard available in most grocery stores is not the same lard that our great-grandmothers used. If you have leaf lard available, then by all means use it for a very finely textured cookie. Otherwise, substitute shortening for lard called for in the recipe.

Flavoring

Vanilla is added to almost any cookie recipe because it enhances the rest of the flavors. You can use rose water to do the same thing and give an old-fashioned flavor. One teaspoon of vanilla and ½ teaspoon of almond extract makes a nice flavor combination for butter cookies and other cookies with a lighter flavor.

Always use pure extracts for the best results. Imitation flavors do not have the same intensity as the natural flavors do. When you invest a little extra money in quality ingredients, you end up with a more delicious product.

Leavening

Leavening is the ingredient that causes baked goods to rise. In breads, it is yeast, and in cakes and cookies, it can be either baking soda or baking powder. It is important to use the leavening called for in the recipe and measure it carefully. Too much baking soda will give your cookies a "soapy" flavor that is not at all appealing. Too much baking powder can give the cookies an acidic flavor.

There are two kinds of baking powder. Single-acting baking powder begins the leavening process when it gets wet. If you are using single-acting baking powder, it is very important to not let the cookie dough sit once the ingredients are mixed. If you don't bake the recipe immediately, the cookies won't rise in the oven and will be like rocks. Double-acting baking powder has two separate processes; the first reacts with moisture, and the second reacts with heat. This allows you to mix up your dough ahead of time without losing any of the rising abilities of the baking powder.

The Art of Measuring and Mixing

Baking cookies is actually a scientific process. Like any other formula, a recipe is written in a certain way to achieve certain results. It is important to read your recipe all the way through before beginning. Make sure you have all the ingredients on hand and in the amounts specified. Mix them in the order given in the recipe instructions. Careful mixing will mean that your cookies come out just the way they are supposed to.

Measure for Accuracy

Accurate measurements mean that your cookies will come out the same, time after time. When you know how to measure accurately, there are no surprises in the finished product. Some people seem to have a knack for adding the right amount of baking powder or salt just by judging the amount. It is a risky way to bake because anyone can have an off day! Here are the methods for measuring different types of ingredients.

- First sift the flour, then spoon it lightly into a measuring cup. Level it off at the top of the cup with a butter knife. Do not pack the flour down.
- To measure sugar, just spoon it into the measuring cup and level off the top.
- Brown sugar is measured by packing it down into the measuring cup. When you tip it out into your recipe, it should keep its shape.
- Confectioners', or powdered, sugar should be sifted before measuring. Spoon it lightly into a measuring cup and level off with a butter knife.
- Measure salt, spices, baking powder, and baking soda by using the measuring spoon to scoop out the ingredient and then level it off gently with a butter knife.
- Cornstarch should be lightly spooned into the measuring cup and then leveled off with a knife. If your recipe calls for a tablespoon or less, use the proper measuring spoon to scoop it out of the container and proceed as with measuring salt.
- To measure flavorings like vanilla, just pour them from the bottle into the properly sized measuring spoon. The liquid should be level with the rim of the spoon.
- Milk, juice, and water are measured by pouring them into the appropriate measuring cup until the liquid is level with the top.
- Oil, honey, and syrup are measured the same way as other liquids. You may need to use a spoon to get all of the ingredient out of the measuring cup.

- Fats are measured by spooning the ingredient into a measuring cup and pressing down firmly to get rid of any air pockets. Sticks of butter generally have the measurements printed on the side of the wrapper in tablespoon increments. One stick, or ¼ pound, of butter is equal to ½ cup.

Mixing the Dough

Nearly every cookie recipe in existence uses the creaming method of mixing the dough. In this technique, the fat and sugar are "creamed" together with a mixer until they are light and fluffy. Generally, the eggs and flavorings are added at this point. Once the eggs are incorporated into the butter mixture, the dry ingredients are stirred in, either by hand or with an electric mixer on low speed.

The dough will mix up better if all the ingredients are at room temperature. The butter should not be melting, but it should not be hard, either. When the eggs are beaten in at room temperature, the texture of the finished cookie is better.

Stir in the sifted dry ingredients carefully. Mix them into the butter mixture until there are no streaks of flour or lumps of baking powder. Be careful not to overmix the dough, or the cookies will be tough. Once the cookie dough is mixed thoroughly, use a wooden spoon to stir in remaining ingredients, like chocolate chips, raisins, and nuts.

Once all ingredients have been mixed, proceed with the recipe according to the instructions.

Sweet Necessities: Equipment and Pans

While it may be true that a poor workman blames his tools, it is also true that using quality equipment makes it easier to create perfect cookies. If at all possible, buy your tools at a restaurant supply store. You will find that commercial pans are less expensive and of higher quality than what is available at a department store.

Having an inventory of good pans and equipment will allow you to bake with confidence at a moment's notice. Some gadgets, like different-sized scoops, are not essential but do make the job easier. Other items, such as cookie presses, are total luxuries but are fun to use.

Essential Equipment

There are some things that you just can't do without when baking cookies. Following is a list of what is needed to make basic cookies. Other items, like cookie cutters, might be essential for fancier cookie baking.

- Two shiny metal baking sheets smaller than your oven's interior. Make sure there is a four-inch space between the edges of the pan and the inside of the oven.
- An electric mixer is the best way to get those ingredients mixed. If you don't have one, you will need a very strong arm and a wooden spoon.
- A couple of mixing bowls allow you to do more than one thing at a time.
- When you have measuring cups and spoons in several sizes, your measurements will be more accurate.
- A glass measuring cup allows for the accurate measuring of liquid ingredients.
- A spatula is necessary for removing cookies from the baking sheet.
- At least one 13″ × 9″ pan is necessary for baking brownies and bars.

Not Essential but Nice to Have

The preceding list includes everything you need to bake many different kinds of basic cookies, but if you want to do anything special, you will need a few more pieces of equipment. Always try to buy the best quality that you can afford. Cheap items just don't last as long or work as well. Faulty equipment can turn your fun afternoon of baking into frustrating work. Good equipment will make your baking easier.

- Cookie cutters in various shapes and sizes are a necessity for cute, decorated sugar cookies. You can find cutters in every shape, from maple leaves to motorcycles.
- Rolling pins are important aids to creating cookies of all kinds. Pick up a few types and choose one that is heavy enough to roll out dough but not so heavy it hurts your back or arms to use it.
- A cookie press allows you to press intricate and beautiful designs into your cookies. Spritz cookies require a good cookie press. Windmill cookies are also traditionally made with a cookie press.
- Pastry tubes and decorating tips allow you to be creative with the cookies that you make.
- A cooling rack allows the cookies to cool on all sides without the bottoms getting soggy.
- A timer will keep you from getting distracted and overbaking the cookies.

- Scoops in various sizes will keep the cookies uniform in size and shape.
- Silpat nonstick baking sheets are made of silicone. You don't need to grease your pans to keep cookies from sticking.

Of course, there are many other items that you could add to the list. But with just some of this equipment, you will be able to make beautiful cookies anytime.

Gilding the Lily: Decorating Tips

There are essentially two types of decorated cookies: the kind that are decorated before baking and the kind that are decorated after baking. The type you use is up to you; there are pros and cons for each. The type that are decorated before baking are usually, although not always, quick to put together. Add a few decorative sprinkles or a bit of sanding sugar, and you are done. Cookies decorated after baking generally take longer and are more intricately done. They are often more beautiful than the simpler cookies. This type of decorating often uses royal icing in different colors, frostings, or even melted chocolate. Depending on the decoration, the process can be tedious, but the results are rewarding.

Here are some tips for beautifully decorated cookies:

- Add food coloring to raw dough for colorful cookies.
- Always let cookies cool completely before decorating.
- Use paste food coloring to color frostings, icings, and white chocolate for the best and most vivid results.
- Royal icing will give the most professional look to your cookies. It dries hard and is durable.
- After decorating your cookies with icing or frosting, set them aside in a safe place until the frosting or icing dries and forms a crust.
- Brush baked and cooled cookies with corn syrup in any pattern and then sprinkle on colored sanding sugar. The corn syrup will make the sugar stick to the patterns.
- Drizzling melted chocolate over a cookie is a wonderful embellishment.
- Dip part of a cookie in melted chocolate and then sprinkle with chopped nuts, decorative sprinkles, or sanding sugar.

Tools for Decorating

You can buy decorating bags made of vinyl or use disposable plastic bags for more convenience. Spoon your frosting into the bag, filling it about halfway. Twist the top of the bag to seal and then squeeze firmly to move the frosting out through the decorating tip and onto your cookie. It will take a bit of practice to become comfortable with the technique. A great way to practice using the different tips is to make designs on a sheet of wax paper.

Some of the tools that you may want to collect are:

- **Couplers**—allow you to change decorating tips quickly and easily
- **Fine writing tips**—great for outlining parts of the cookie, making scrolls and small dots, and writing star tips
- **Larger writing tips**—great for polka dots and filling in larger areas with color
- **Toothpicks**—can be used to move color or create a chevron effect when you drag them through stripes of thin frosting

Once the cookies are decorated, set them aside to allow the frosting to harden before storing; this will keep the designs from smearing. A final garnish may be created by using products like luster dust or edible glitter to enhance the decorated cookie. Some people even use edible gold leaf for very special decorated cookies.

Royal icing stores and ships well once it hardens, but buttercream does not. It is best to decorate cookies with buttercream just before serving. If you are making cookies that will be stored for a period of time or shipped, use royal icing and allow it to harden completely before packing and shipping. The icing will help seal the cookie and maintain the fresh flavor and texture.

Storing Cookies

All cookies have different techniques for successful storage. Always allow cookies, brownies, and bars to cool completely before packaging them for storage. If you have decorated the cookies, take the time to allow the icing to harden before you try to store them. This will keep them as beautiful as they were when you first made them. Any cookies that are properly stored should keep close to 1 week at room temperature.

Crisp cookies should be stored in a container that is loosely covered. This allows the moisture to be released from the container easily, stopping it from building up and making cookies soggy. If you live in an area with high humidity, it is actually better to store cookies in an airtight container to keep the moisture out.

Soft cookies should be kept in an airtight container. This traps the moisture in with the cookies, keeping them soft and chewy. If they begin to dry out, you can add a slice of apple or a piece of bread to the container. Always keep an eye on soft cookies because they tend to get moldy more quickly than crisp ones. Separating layers of cookies with wax paper will keep them from sticking to each other and make them easy to remove from the container.

When cookies are iced, they should also be kept in an airtight container. Allow the icing to harden completely and layer the cookies between sheets of wax paper. Do not make more than three layers in a container because the weight will cause the bottom layers to crumble and the icings to crack.

For long-term storage, cookies can be easily frozen. You can freeze the dough for up to 12 months or baked cookies for up to 6 months. Never freeze more than one kind of dough or cookie together—the different cookies will take on each other's flavors. Always wrap the cookies or dough in several layers of plastic wrap and then put them in an airtight container to prevent the cookies from picking up the flavor of other foods in the freezer.

Baked cookies can be put in freezer bags and frozen, but this often results in a lot of broken cookies. It is better to layer them in a freezer container with wax paper between the layers and over the top. The sturdy container will support the cookies, and they will be less likely to crumble. Label the container with the type of cookie and the date they were frozen so you can keep track of them.

If you freeze crisp cookies and then find that when they have thawed they are no longer as crisp as you would like, you can restore the crispness by warming them up in a 300°F oven for about 5 minutes.

Time for Cookies!

Baking delicious cookies should be fun, easy, and accessible—and these qualities are exactly what you'll find in the recipes in the following chapters. Take your time and read the entire recipe before you start; knowing what's ahead helps you to prepare your ingredients, your equipment, and your schedule—some recipes require chill times of an hour or more. So grab your apron! It's time to bake some cookies!

CHAPTER 2
Drop Cookies

Drop cookies are quick and easy to make; just mix up the dough, scoop it onto a cookie sheet, and pop them in the oven. This chapter includes your favorite chip cookies, like Classic Chocolate Chip, Oatmeal Chocolate Chip, and White Chocolate Chip Macadamia, and other favorites like Whoopie Pies, M&M's Cookies, and Vanilla Wafers. And don't miss the Cookies 'N' Cream Cookies, Red Velvet White Chocolate Chip, and Oatmeal Cream Pies.

Brown Butter Toffee Chocolate Chip Cookies

YIELDS
20
COOKIES

Brown butter transforms the flavor of these cookies, adding a deep caramelized, nutty flavor that regular butter cannot achieve on its own. These cookies are crispy, chewy, salty, and sweet! Be sure to allow the brown butter to cool for 20 minutes and chill your dough for 30 minutes.

Recipe Prep Time: 1 hour

Recipe Cook Time: 14 minutes

1 cup unsalted butter

1 cup packed dark brown sugar

⅓ cup granulated sugar

2 large eggs

2 teaspoons vanilla extract

1 cup all-purpose flour

1 cup whole-wheat flour

1 teaspoon baking soda

1 teaspoon salt

½ cup Heath Toffee Bits

1½ cups semisweet chocolate chunks

1 teaspoon flakey sea salt

1. Preheat oven to 350°F. Line two baking sheets with parchment.

2. In a medium saucepan over medium heat, add butter. As butter melts, continuously swirl over heat until it begins to brown and foam, about 5–8 minutes. Set aside to cool for 20 minutes.

3. In a large bowl, use an electric mixer on medium speed to beat butter, brown sugar, granulated sugar, and eggs until fluffy. Mix in vanilla and continue to beat until mixture lightens.

4. In a medium bowl, whisk all-purpose flour, whole-wheat flour, baking soda, and salt until well combined.

5. Mix flour mixture into butter mixture until well incorporated. Mix in toffee bits and chocolate chunks. Allow dough to chill about 30 minutes, as this will prevent cookies from flattening.

6. When ready to bake, drop dough by rounded teaspoons about 2" apart onto prepared sheets. Bake 9–11 minutes. Sprinkle with sea salt. Cool on sheets 10 minutes before removing. Serve.

Per Serving (Serving size: 1 cookie):
Calories: 285 • Fat: 15g • Sodium: 300mg • Carbohydrates: 36g • Fiber: 2g • Sugar: 25g
Protein: 3g

Classic Chocolate Chip

YIELDS 24 COOKIES

These cookies are the recipe everyone craves—a crisp outside with a chewy middle. Take these out of the oven when they are still slightly underdone for best results.

Recipe Prep Time: 10 minutes
Recipe Cook Time: 8 minutes

½ cup unsalted butter, softened
½ cup vegetable shortening
¾ cup granulated sugar
¾ cup packed light brown sugar
2 large eggs
1 tablespoon vanilla extract
2¼ cups all-purpose flour
1 teaspoon baking soda
2 cups semisweet chocolate chips

1. Preheat oven to 350°F. Lightly grease two baking sheets.

2. In a large bowl, use an electric mixer on medium speed to cream butter, shortening, granulated sugar, and brown sugar until fluffy. Add eggs one at a time, beating well after each egg is added. Beat in vanilla.

3. In a medium bowl, combine flour and baking soda. Stir into butter mixture. Carefully fold in chocolate chips.

4. Drop dough by rounded teaspoons about 2" apart onto prepared sheets. Bake 8–10 minutes until edges are just lightly brown. Cool on sheets 10 minutes before removing. Serve.

Per Serving (Serving size: 1 cookie):
Calories: 244 • Fat: 12g • Sodium: 62mg • Carbohydrates: 32g • Fiber: 1g • Sugar: 21g
Protein: 2g

Double Chocolate Chip Cookies

YIELDS 24 COOKIES

These are the ultimate cookie for chocolate lovers! They're sweet, chewy, decadent, and loaded with cocoa flavor. Be sure to use natural 100% cocoa powder, such as Hershey's cocoa powder. Adding espresso powder enhances the flavor even more.

Recipe Prep Time: 10 minutes

Recipe Cook Time: 8 minutes

1 cup unsalted butter, softened

½ cup granulated sugar

2 large eggs

2 teaspoons vanilla extract

1½ cups all-purpose flour

½ teaspoon salt

¾ teaspoon baking soda

½ cup cocoa powder

1 teaspoon espresso powder

2 cups semisweet chocolate chips

1. Preheat oven to 350°F. Lightly grease two baking sheets or line with parchment.

2. In a large bowl, use an electric mixer on medium speed to beat butter, sugar, and eggs until fluffy. Mix in vanilla.

3. In a medium bowl, mix flour, salt, baking soda, cocoa powder, and espresso powder and whisk until combined.

4. Slowly add flour mixture to butter mixture, mixing until just combined. Fold in chocolate chips carefully.

5. Drop dough by rounded teaspoons about 2" apart onto prepared sheets. Bake 8–10 minutes. Cool on sheets about 10 minutes before removing. Serve.

Per Serving (Serving size: 1 cookie):
Calories: 196 • Fat: 12g • Sodium: 96mg • Carbohydrates: 21g • Fiber: 2g • Sugar: 13g
Protein: 2g

Red Velvet White Chocolate Chip

YIELDS
20
COOKIES

You've got to try these incredible cookies. If you prefer a stronger chocolate taste, add an additional teaspoon or two of cocoa powder. Keep in mind that adding more cocoa will take away from the vibrant red color. For a professional-looking finish, press a few extra white chips into the tops of the cookies as soon as you remove them from the oven.

Recipe Prep Time: **10 minutes**

Recipe Cook Time: **8 minutes**

½ cup unsalted butter, softened
½ cup granulated sugar
¼ cup packed dark brown sugar
1 large egg
2 teaspoons vanilla extract
1½ teaspoons red gel food coloring
1⅓ cups all-purpose flour
5 teaspoons cocoa powder
½ teaspoon baking soda
½ teaspoon salt
1 cup white chocolate chips

1. Preheat oven to 350°F. Lightly grease two baking sheets or line with parchment.

2. In a large bowl, use an electric mixer on medium speed to cream butter, granulated sugar, and brown sugar until fluffy. Add egg, vanilla, and food coloring until well combined.

3. In a separate large bowl, whisk together flour, cocoa, baking soda, and salt.

4. Slowly add flour mixture to butter mixture. Fold in white chocolate chips.

5. Drop dough by rounded teaspoons about 2″ apart onto prepared sheets. Bake 8–10 minutes until edges are crispy. Cool on sheets 10 minutes before removing. Serve.

Per Serving (Serving size: 1 cookie):
Calories: 153 • Fat: 7g • Sodium: 102mg • Carbohydrates: 20g • Fiber: 0g • Sugar: 13g
Protein: 2g

Lavender White Chocolate Drops

YIELDS
36
COOKIES

These gorgeous cookies, with their flecks of purple, are social media–worthy! Lavender has a citrus flavor that should be used sparingly; too much causes a bitter taste. And always be sure to use food-grade lavender flowers.

Recipe Prep Time: **15 minutes**
Recipe Cook Time: **8 minutes**

½ cup vegetable shortening
½ cup unsalted butter
½ cup packed light brown sugar
1 cup granulated sugar
2 large eggs
1 tablespoon vanilla extract
1 tablespoon grated lemon peel
2¼ cups all-purpose flour
1 teaspoon baking soda
1 tablespoon dried food-grade
    lavender flowers
2 cups white chocolate chunks
    or chips

1. Preheat oven to 350°F. Line two baking sheets with parchment.

2. In a large bowl, use an electric mixer on medium speed to cream shortening, butter, brown sugar, and granulated sugar until light and fluffy. Beat in eggs, vanilla, and lemon peel.

3. In a medium bowl, combine flour and baking soda. Stir into butter mixture until well blended.

4. Stir in lavender and white chocolate.

5. Drop dough by rounded teaspoons onto prepared sheets and bake 8–10 minutes until lightly brown on the edges.

6. Cool on sheets 5 minutes before removing to finish cooling to room temperature. Serve.

Per Serving (Serving size: 1 cookie):
Calories: 165 • Fat: 8g • Sodium: 48mg • Carbohydrates: 20g • Fiber: 0g • Sugar: 14g
Protein: 2g

Butterscotch Cookies

YIELDS **24** COOKIES

Butter and brown sugar—what's not to love about these scrumptious cookies? Butterscotch is a classic and delicious flavor. The pecans add a nice depth of flavor and texture. Be sure to use whole buttermilk in this recipe, not skim or low-fat.

Recipe Prep Time: **10 minutes**

Recipe Cook Time: **10 minutes**

1¼ cups all-purpose flour

½ teaspoon baking soda

¼ teaspoon baking powder

¼ teaspoon salt

¼ cup unsalted butter, softened

¾ cup packed dark brown sugar

1 large egg

1 teaspoon vanilla extract

½ cup whole buttermilk

½ cup chopped pecans

1. Preheat oven to 350°F. Lightly grease two baking sheets.

2. In a medium bowl, combine flour, baking soda, baking powder, and salt. Set aside.

3. In a large bowl, use an electric mixer on medium speed to cream butter and brown sugar until light and fluffy. Beat in egg and vanilla.

4. Add flour mixture to butter mixture, alternating with buttermilk, mixing well after each addition. Stir in pecans.

5. Drop dough by rounded teaspoons about 2″ apart onto prepared sheets. Bake 10–12 minutes until golden brown; do not overbake. Cool on sheets a few minutes before removing. Serve.

Per Serving (Serving size: 1 cookie):
Calories: 88 • Fat: 4g • Sodium: 66mg • Carbohydrates: 12g • Fiber: 0g • Sugar: 7g Protein: 1g

Whoopie Pies

YIELDS
16
PIES

Whoopie Pies are oversized sandwich cookies that consist of two soft, cake-like cookies and a cream filling. They are a traditional Pennsylvania Dutch treat popular throughout Pennsylvania and New England. The finished cookies need to be stored in the refrigerator to keep the cream filling fresh.

Recipe Prep Time: **20 minutes**
Recipe Cook Time: **10 minutes**

Cookies

2⅔ cups all-purpose flour
½ cup Hershey's Special Dark cocoa
1 teaspoon baking powder
1 teaspoon baking soda
1 teaspoon salt
½ cup hot coffee
½ cup sour milk
1½ cups granulated sugar
½ cup vegetable shortening
2 large eggs
1 teaspoon vanilla extract

Filling

1 cup whole milk
¼ cup all-purpose flour
1 cup granulated sugar
1 teaspoon vanilla extract
½ cup unsalted butter, softened
½ cup vegetable shortening

1. Preheat oven to 350°F. Lightly grease two baking sheets.

2. To make Cookies: In a large bowl, combine flour, cocoa, baking powder, baking soda, and salt and set aside.

3. In a small bowl, combine coffee and sour milk and set aside.

4. In a separate large bowl, beat sugar and shortening until fluffy. Add eggs and vanilla and blend well. Starting with the flour mixture, add dry ingredients and sour milk mixture alternately, ending with flour.

5. Drop dough by rounded tablespoons onto prepared sheets. Flatten slightly with wet fingertips. (You should get thirty-two Cookies.)

6. Bake 10–12 minutes or until Cookies spring back when lightly touched. Cool completely before filling.

7. To make Filling: In a medium microwave-safe bowl, mix milk and flour and microwave on high for 1-minute increments, stirring in between until mixture becomes paste-like. Chill mixture until cool.

8. In a third large bowl, beat sugar, vanilla, butter, and shortening until fluffy. Add cooled flour mixture and beat until mixture is light and airy. It should double in volume. Chill.

9. Place a spoonful of Filling on flat side of one Cookie and top with another, with flat side toward Filling, to create a sandwich. Serve.

Per Serving (Serving size: 1 pie):
Calories: 398 • Fat: 19g • Sodium: 275mg • Carbohydrates: 51g • Fiber: 1g • Sugar: 33g Protein: 4g

Oatmeal Cream Pies

YIELDS
20
PIES

These classic cookies are very similar to Whoopie Pies and have the same filling, but the cookie is a bit more prone to crumbling, so handle with care. As with Whoopie Pies, these finished cookies must be refrigerated.

Recipe Prep Time: **20 minutes**
Recipe Cook Time: **10 minutes**

½ cup unsalted butter, softened
¼ cup vegetable shortening
2 cups packed light brown sugar
2 large eggs
1 teaspoon baking soda
3 tablespoons boiling water
½ teaspoon salt
2 cups all-purpose flour
2 cups quick-cooking oats
1 teaspoon ground cinnamon
1 teaspoon baking powder
Cream Filling for Whoopie Pies
     (see recipe in this chapter)

1. Preheat oven to 350°F. Line two baking sheets with parchment.

2. In a large bowl, use an electric mixer on medium speed to cream butter, shortening, and brown sugar until fluffy. Add eggs and beat well.

3. In a small bowl, combine baking soda and water. Add to butter mixture, beating in carefully.

4. In a separate large bowl, combine salt, flour, oats, cinnamon, and baking powder. Stir flour mixture into butter and baking soda mixture.

5. Drop dough by rounded tablespoons onto prepared sheets. (You should get forty cookies.) Bake 10–12 minutes until golden brown. Cool completely.

6. Make the Whoopie Pies filling.

7. To assemble the pies, place a spoonful of filling on flat side of one cookie and top with another, with flat side toward filling, to create a sandwich. Serve or store in an airtight container in the refrigerator for up to 1 week.

Per Serving (Serving size: 1 pie):
Calories: 368 · Fat: 17g · Sodium: 237mg · Carbohydrates: 49g · Fiber: 1g · Sugar: 32g
Protein: 4g

Pumpkin Whoopie Pies

YIELDS 18 PIES

These are delicious all year long, but they are a special treat when the first crisp breezes of autumn start pulling the leaves from the trees. The mellow pumpkin flavors of the cookie are brought out by the candied ginger and cream cheese in the filling. If candied ginger is not available, you can substitute ¼ teaspoon powdered ginger.

Recipe Prep Time: 15 minutes

Recipe Cook Time: 10 minutes

Cookies

3 cups all-purpose flour
1 teaspoon baking powder
1 teaspoon baking soda
1 teaspoon salt
1½ teaspoons ground cinnamon
1 teaspoon ground ginger
½ teaspoon ground cloves
½ teaspoon freshly grated nutmeg
2½ cups packed light brown sugar
1 cup vegetable oil
2 large eggs
2 cups solid-packed pure pumpkin
1 teaspoon vanilla extract

Filling

4 tablespoons unsalted butter, softened
4 ounces cream cheese
1 cup confectioners' sugar
½ teaspoon vanilla extract
2 tablespoons minced candied ginger

1. Preheat oven to 350°F.

2. To make Cookies: In a large mixing bowl, combine flour, baking powder, baking soda, salt, cinnamon, ground ginger, cloves, and nutmeg. Set aside.

3. In a separate large bowl, use an electric mixer on medium speed to cream brown sugar, oil, eggs, pumpkin, and vanilla until fluffy.

4. Add flour mixture to pumpkin mixture and mix well.

5. Drop dough by rounded tablespoons onto two ungreased baking sheets. (You should get thirty-six Cookies.) Bake 10–12 minutes. When done, centers of Cookies will spring back when lightly touched.

6. Cool thoroughly before filling.

7. To make Filling: In a third large bowl, use an electric mixer on medium speed to beat butter and cream cheese until fluffy. Add confectioners' sugar, vanilla, and candied ginger. Beat until fluffy.

8. To assemble the pies, place a spoonful of Filling on flat side of one Cookie and top with another, with flat side toward filling, to create a sandwich. Serve or store in an airtight container in the refrigerator for up to 1 week.

Per Serving (Serving size: 1 pie):
Calories: 394 • Fat: 17g • Sodium: 267mg • Carbohydrates: 56g • Fiber: 1g • Sugar: 38g Protein: 4g

Cookies 'N' Cream Cookies

YIELDS **30** COOKIES

The combination of butter and cream cheese gives these cookies the perfect chewy bite and uniquely creamy flavor. The dough is loaded with large chunks of Oreos and white chocolate chips. Use semisweet chips if you prefer. The cornstarch makes these cookies extra fluffy.

Recipe Prep Time: **15 minutes**
Recipe Cook Time: **10 minutes**

¾ cup unsalted butter, softened
4 ounces cream cheese
½ cup packed light brown sugar
½ cup granulated sugar
1 large egg
1 teaspoon vanilla extract
2¼ cups all-purpose flour
1 teaspoon cornstarch
1 teaspoon baking soda
1 teaspoon salt
12 Oreo sandwich cookies
1 cup white chocolate chips

1. Preheat oven to 350°F. Line two baking sheets with parchment.

2. In a large bowl, use an electric mixer on medium speed to cream butter, cream cheese, brown sugar, and granulated sugar until light and fluffy. Beat in egg and vanilla.

3. In a separate large bowl, whisk together flour, cornstarch, baking soda, and salt. Add in increments to the cream cheese mixture.

4. Place Oreos in a zip-top plastic bag. Use a rolling pin to crush them to pieces about the size of a chocolate chip. Don't crush them too fine.

5. Fold Oreos and white chocolate chips into the batter.

6. Drop dough by rounded teaspoons onto prepared sheets. Bake 10–12 minutes or until edges are golden and crispy.

7. Cool on sheets 5 minutes before removing. Serve.

Per Serving (Serving size: 1 cookie):
Calories: 170 • Fat: 8g • Sodium: 161mg • Carbohydrates: 21g • Fiber: 0g • Sugar: 12g
Protein: 2g

Glazed Ginger Creams

YIELDS **36** COOKIES

With a flavor reminiscent of gingersnaps, these spicy cookies are the perfect ending to a chilly day. They are softer and more cake-like than gingersnaps.

Recipe Prep Time: **10 minutes**
Recipe Cook Time: **20 minutes**

Cookies

½ cup granulated sugar
¼ cup vegetable shortening
1 large egg
¼ cup unsulfured molasses
½ teaspoon baking soda
½ cup hot black coffee
1½ cups all-purpose flour
½ teaspoon ground ginger
½ teaspoon ground cinnamon
½ teaspoon ground cloves
½ cup raisins
⅛ cup finely chopped crystallized ginger

Glaze

Juice and grated rind of 1 medium orange
1 cup confectioners' sugar, plus more
*   if needed*

1. Preheat oven to 350°F. Lightly grease two baking sheets.

2. To make Cookies: In a large bowl, use an electric mixer on medium speed to cream granulated sugar and shortening until light and fluffy. Add egg and mix well. Stir in molasses.

3. In a small bowl, dissolve baking soda in coffee. Stir into shortening mixture.

4. Combine flour, ginger, cinnamon, and cloves and stir into shortening-coffee mixture. Fold in raisins and crystallized ginger.

5. Drop dough by rounded teaspoons onto prepared sheets. Bake 20 minutes until golden brown.

6. To make Glaze: In a small bowl, mix juice and grated rind with confectioners' sugar. If the Glaze is too liquidy and not spreadable, add additional confectioners' sugar until you reach the desired consistency. Spread Glaze over Cookies while they are warm and let sit at room temperature. Serve.

Per Serving (Serving size: 1 cookie):
Calories: 72 · Fat: 2g · Sodium: 20mg · Carbohydrates: 14g · Fiber: 0g · Sugar: 9g Protein: 1g

Classic Oatmeal Cookies

YIELDS
30
COOKIES

Chewy and delicious, these cookies are loved by kids of all ages. Leave them plain or add a cup of raisins, a cup of shredded coconut, a cup of chopped pecans (or walnuts), or add all three of these extras. Incorporate any add-ins after you've fully mixed the dry ingredients into the wet ingredients. Be careful not to over-bake these or they will be too hard.

Recipe Prep Time: **10 minutes**

Recipe Cook Time: **12 minutes**

6 tablespoons vegetable shortening

½ cup packed light brown sugar

¼ cup granulated sugar

1 large egg

½ teaspoon vanilla extract

⅛ cup water

1½ cups old-fashioned oats

½ cup all-purpose flour

½ teaspoon salt

¼ teaspoon baking soda

1. Preheat oven to 350°F. Lightly grease two baking sheets.

2. In a large bowl, use an electric mixer on medium speed to beat shortening, brown sugar, and granulated sugar until light and fluffy. Beat in egg, vanilla, and water.

3. In a separate large bowl, combine oats, flour, salt, and baking soda. Stir oats mixture into shortening mixture.

4. Drop dough by rounded teaspoons onto prepared sheets. Bake 12–15 minutes until just golden brown.

5. Cool on sheets 5 minutes before removing. Serve.

Per Serving (Serving size: 1 cookie):
Calories: 68 • Fat: 3g • Sodium: 52mg • Carbohydrates: 10g • Fiber: 0g • Sugar: 5g
Protein: 1g

Oatmeal Chocolate Chip

These Oatmeal Chocolate Chip cookies have the perfect texture and bite. If you have a hard time choosing between oatmeal raisin and oatmeal chocolate chip, the chocolate chips in this recipe can easily be replaced with raisins if you prefer.

Recipe Prep Time: 30 minutes

Recipe Cook Time: 8 minutes

1 cup all-purpose flour
½ teaspoon baking soda
½ teaspoon salt
1 teaspoon ground cinnamon
½ cup unsalted butter, softened
⅔ cup packed dark brown sugar
⅓ cup granulated sugar
1 large egg
2 teaspoons vanilla extract
1½ cups old-fashioned oats
1 cup semisweet chocolate chips
½ cup chopped walnuts

1. Preheat oven to 375°F. Lightly grease two baking sheets or line with parchment.

2. In a medium bowl, whisk together flour, baking soda, salt, and cinnamon. Set aside.

3. In a large bowl, use an electric mixer on medium speed to cream butter, brown sugar, and granulated sugar and beat until well combined. Add egg and vanilla and continue to mix well.

4. Slowly add flour mixture to butter mixture and mix until just combined.

5. Stir in oats, chocolate chips, and walnuts. Allow dough to chill 20 minutes.

6. Drop dough by rounded teaspoons onto prepared sheets. Bake 8–10 minutes until edges are golden brown and center is soft and chewy. Cool and serve.

Per Serving (Serving size: 1 cookie):
Calories: 162 • Fat: 8g • Sodium: 80mg • Carbohydrates: 21g • Fiber: 1g • Sugar: 13g
Protein: 2g

Black Forest Cookies

YIELDS
36
COOKIES

Dark chocolate, cherries, and a creamy frosting—everything you love about a Black Forest cake in a cookie. For extra flavor, try soaking the dried cherries in kirsch before adding them to the batter. If your frosting is too thick once all of the confectioners' sugar has been used, add up to 1 tablespoon of heavy cream to thin it out a little. Store cookies in an airtight container in the refrigerator up to 1 week.

Recipe Prep Time: 25 minutes, plus 30 minutes chill time

Recipe Cook Time: 10 minutes

Cookies

1 cup all-purpose flour

¼ cup Hershey's Special Dark cocoa

1 teaspoon baking powder

⅛ teaspoon salt

1 cup chopped bittersweet chocolate

½ cup unsalted butter

¾ cup granulated sugar

2 large eggs

1 cup dried cherries

2 cups dark chocolate chunks

1 cup coarsely chopped bittersweet chocolate, for garnish

Cream Cheese Frosting

8 ounces full-fat cream cheese

⅓ cup unsalted butter, softened

3 teaspoons vanilla extract

4 cups confectioners' sugar

1. Preheat oven to 350°F. Line two baking sheets with parchment.

2. To make Cookies: In a large bowl, stir together flour, cocoa, baking powder, and salt until combined.

3. In a small saucepan over low heat, melt bittersweet chocolate and butter until smooth. Remove from heat, transfer to a large bowl, and allow to cool to room temperature.

4. Beat sugar and eggs into chocolate mixture until very smooth. Stir in flour mixture until blended, but do not overmix. Add cherries and chocolate chunks. Chill mixture 30 minutes.

5. Drop dough by rounded teaspoons onto prepared sheets. Bake 10 minutes; do not overbake. Cool 5 minutes on sheets and then remove to cool completely.

6. To make Cream Cheese Frosting: In a separate large bowl, use an electric mixer on medium speed to mix cream cheese and butter until well blended. Beat in vanilla.

7. Slowly beat in confectioners' sugar until proper consistency is reached.

8. Frost tops of Cookies and then garnish with chopped chocolate. Serve.

Per Serving (Serving size: 1 cookie):
Calories: 256 • Fat: 12g • Sodium: 54mg • Carbohydrates: 34g • Fiber: 2g • Sugar: 27g
Protein: 2g

Matcha White Chocolate Chip Cookies

YIELDS 12 COOKIES

These cookies are crisp around the edges with a soft and chewy center. The matcha adds a unique, earthy flavor that is balanced by the white chocolate and vanilla. If you prefer a more intense matcha flavor, add an additional teaspoon to the recipe. You can also make these with any other baking chips such as semi-sweet, dark chocolate, or milk chocolate.

Recipe Prep Time: 10 minutes

Recipe Cook Time: 8 minutes

½ cup unsalted butter
¼ cup packed dark brown sugar
½ cup granulated sugar
1 large egg
1 large egg yolk
½ teaspoon vanilla extract
1⅔ cups all-purpose flour
2½ teaspoons matcha powder
½ teaspoon baking soda
½ teaspoon baking powder
¼ teaspoon salt
¾ cup white chocolate chips

1. Preheat oven to 350°F. Lightly grease a baking sheet or line with parchment.

2. In a large bowl, use an electric mixer on medium speed to cream butter, brown sugar, and granulated sugar until fluffy. Add egg, egg yolk, and vanilla and beat well.

3. In a medium bowl, mix flour, matcha powder, baking soda, baking powder, and salt. Add dry mixture to butter mixture and combine.

4. Carefully fold in white chocolate chips.

5. Drop dough by teaspoons about 2″ apart onto prepared sheet. Bake 8–10 minutes until edges are golden brown. Cool on sheet 10 minutes before removing. Serve.

Per Serving (Serving size: 1 cookie):
Calories: 232 • Fat: 11g • Sodium: 86mg • Carbohydrates: 30g • Fiber: 1g • Sugar: 19g
Protein: 3g

Blueberry White Chocolate Chippers

YIELDS 24 COOKIES

These cookies are bursting with flavor from blueberries, lemon, nutmeg, and white chocolate. If you like spiced cookies, replace the lemon peel with finely chopped candied ginger.

Recipe Prep Time: **10 minutes**

Recipe Cook Time: **8 minutes**

¼ cup unsalted butter, softened
¼ cup vegetable shortening
6 tablespoons granulated sugar
6 tablespoons packed light brown sugar
1 large egg
½ teaspoon vanilla extract
1 tablespoon grated lemon peel
1⅛ cups all-purpose flour
⅛ teaspoon freshly grated nutmeg
½ teaspoon baking soda
¼ teaspoon salt
½ cup dried blueberries
¾ cup white chocolate chips

1. Preheat oven to 350°F. Line two baking sheets with parchment.

2. In a large bowl, use an electric mixer on medium speed to cream butter, shortening, granulated sugar, and brown sugar. Add egg, vanilla, and lemon peel and beat until well blended.

3. In a separate large bowl, mix flour, nutmeg, baking soda, and salt. Add to butter mixture and blend well. Fold in blueberries and white chocolate chips.

4. Drop dough by rounded teaspoons about 2″ apart onto prepared sheets. Bake 8–10 minutes, removing from oven when just barely brown.

5. Cool on sheets 5 minutes before removing to a cooling rack to cool completely. Serve.

Per Serving (Serving size: 1 cookie):
Calories: 124 • Fat: 6g • Sodium: 59mg • Carbohydrates: 17g • Fiber: 0g • Sugar: 12g
Protein: 1g

Mudslides

YIELDS 24 COOKIES

These cookies are so chocolaty, it is almost overwhelming. When melting chocolate, be sure that your equipment is clean and dry. Even the smallest amount of water in your chocolate will make it impossible to work with. For best results, microwave chocolate on low heat, stirring every minute or so until the chocolate is soft. Remove from the microwave and continue to stir until chocolate has melted completely.

Recipe Prep Time: **15 minutes**
Recipe Cook Time: **8 minutes**

2 ounces unsweetened chocolate, roughly chopped

4 ounces bittersweet chocolate, roughly chopped

4 ounces semisweet chocolate, roughly chopped

2 tablespoons plus 2 teaspoons unsalted butter

⅓ cup all-purpose flour

1 teaspoon baking powder

¼ teaspoon salt

3 large eggs

¾ cup plus 2 tablespoons granulated sugar

½ teaspoon vanilla extract

½ teaspoon strong espresso

1 cup milk chocolate chips

1. Preheat oven to 400°F. Line two baking sheets with parchment.

2. In a medium microwave-safe bowl, melt unsweetened chocolate, bittersweet chocolate, and semisweet chocolate with butter in microwave on low in 1-minute increments. Stir every minute until smooth.

3. In a medium bowl, sift together flour, baking powder, and salt. Set aside.

4. In a large bowl, use an electric mixer on medium speed to beat eggs, sugar, vanilla, espresso, and melted chocolate until light and fluffy.

5. Add flour mixture to egg mixture and blend until just combined. Stir in chocolate chips.

6. Drop dough by rounded teaspoons onto prepared sheets. Bake 8 minutes, being careful not to overbake. The tops will be cracked. Cool and serve.

Per Serving (Serving size: 1 cookie):
Calories: 169 • Fat: 8g • Sodium: 49mg • Carbohydrates: 21g • Fiber: 1g • Sugar: 17g
Protein: 2g

Vanilla Wafers

YIELDS
24
COOKIES

An easy way to get these shaped and sized correctly is to use a pastry bag and pipe the dough onto the baking sheets. Make them quarter-sized for the best results. You can also make colored cookies by separating the dough into several bowls and adding different food coloring to each.

Recipe Prep Time: 10 minutes

Recipe Cook Time: 12 minutes

½ cup unsalted butter, softened

1 cup granulated sugar

1 large egg

1 tablespoon vanilla extract

1⅓ cups all-purpose flour

¾ teaspoon baking soda

¼ teaspoon salt

1. Preheat oven to 350°F.

2. In a large bowl, use an electric mixer on medium speed to cream butter and sugar until fluffy. Beat in egg and vanilla.

3. In a medium bowl, combine flour, baking soda, and salt. Stir into butter mixture.

4. Drop dough by rounded teaspoons onto two ungreased baking sheets.

5. Bake 12–15 minutes or until edges are brown. Cool and serve.

Per Serving (Serving size: 1 cookie):
Calories: 107 • Fat: 4g • Sodium: 78mg • Carbohydrates: 14g • Fiber: 0g • Sugar: 8g
Protein: 2g

S'mores Cookies

YIELDS
20
COOKIES

Now you can have incredible S'mores Cookies with no campfire necessary! These cookies are loaded with graham cracker crumbles and gooey marshmallows. As the cookies bake, the marshmallows puff up, creating the most delicious chewy cookie.

Recipe Prep Time: **12 minutes**

Recipe Cook Time: **10 minutes**

10 tablespoons unsalted butter, softened
½ cup packed light brown sugar
¼ cup granulated sugar
1 large egg
1½ teaspoons vanilla extract
1½ cups all-purpose flour
½ teaspoon baking powder
½ teaspoon baking soda
½ teaspoon salt
¾ cup semisweet chocolate chips
1 cup mini marshmallows, divided
6 graham crackers, crushed to large
    crumbs
2 (1.55-ounce) Hershey's milk chocolate
    candy bars, broken into squares

1. Preheat oven to 350°F. Line two baking sheets with parchment.

2. In a large bowl, use an electric mixer on medium speed to beat butter, brown sugar, granulated sugar, egg, and vanilla until combined.

3. In a separate large bowl, combine flour, baking powder, baking soda, and salt. Stir into butter mixture.

4. Fold in chocolate chips, marshmallows (reserving ⅛ cup), and crushed graham crackers.

5. Drop dough in mounds, about 2 tablespoons in size and about 2" apart, onto prepared sheets. Bake 8 minutes.

6. Remove cookies and gently press one or two pieces of candy bars and a few remaining marshmallows into the top of each cookie. Place cookies back into oven for an additional 2–3 minutes to finish baking.

7. Cool completely before removing from sheets. Serve.

Per Serving (Serving size: 1 cookie):
Calories: 160 • Fat: 8g • Sodium: 110mg • Carbohydrates: 22g • Fiber: 1g • Sugar: 13g
Protein: 2g

Carrot Cake Cookies

YIELDS
36
COOKIES

These cookies taste remarkably like carrot cake. Their flavor improves after standing, so allow them to mellow for at least a day before enjoying them. Add the Cream Cheese Frosting from the Black Forest Cookies (see recipe in this chapter) for an even more cake-like experience. Frosted cookies should be stored in an airtight container in the refrigerator for up to 1 week.

Recipe Prep Time: 10 minutes

Recipe Cook Time: 15 minutes

½ cup unsalted butter, softened

1 cup packed light brown sugar

2 large eggs

1 teaspoon vanilla extract

1 (8-ounce) can crushed pineapple,
*   well drained*

¾ cup grated carrots

1 cup raisins

2 cups all-purpose flour

1 teaspoon baking powder

½ teaspoon baking soda

½ teaspoon salt

2 tablespoons ground cinnamon

½ teaspoon ground cloves

¼ teaspoon ground ginger

½ cup white chocolate chips

1 cup chopped walnuts

1. Preheat oven to 350°F. Line two baking sheets with parchment.

2. In a large bowl, use an electric mixer on medium speed to cream butter and brown sugar until fluffy. Beat in eggs and vanilla.

3. Stir in pineapple, carrots, and raisins.

4. In a separate large bowl, whisk together flour, baking powder, baking soda, salt, cinnamon, cloves, and ginger. Blend into butter mixture. Stir in white chocolate chips and walnuts.

5. Drop dough by rounded teaspoons onto prepared sheets. Bake 15–20 minutes until golden brown. Cool and serve.

_____

Per Serving (Serving size: 1 cookie):
Calories: 128 • Fat: 5g • Sodium: 73mg • Carbohydrates: 18g • Fiber: 1g • Sugar: 11g
Protein: 2g

Chubby Hubby Cookies

YIELDS
30
COOKIES

These big cookies are bursting with sweet *and* salty flavors—the best of both worlds! When crushing the pretzels, break them into small chunks about the size of chocolate chips.

Recipe Prep Time: **10 minutes**
Recipe Cook Time: **10 minutes**

1 cup unsalted butter, softened
½ cup granulated sugar
½ cup packed light brown sugar
1 large egg
1 tablespoon vanilla extract
2 cups all-purpose flour
½ tablespoon baking soda
6 ounces semisweet chocolate chips
6 ounces peanut butter chips
½ cup chopped salted peanuts
1 cup coarsely crushed pretzels

1. Preheat oven to 350°F.

2. In a large bowl, use an electric mixer on medium speed to cream butter, granulated sugar, and brown sugar until light and fluffy. Blend in egg, then vanilla.

3. In a medium bowl, whisk together flour and baking soda. Stir into butter mixture.

4. Stir in chocolate chips, peanut butter chips, chopped peanuts, and crushed pretzels.

5. Drop dough by heaping tablespoons onto two ungreased baking sheets. Bake 10–13 minutes. Edges will be firm, but middles will still be soft. Cool a few minutes on sheets before removing. Serve.

Per Serving (Serving size: 1 cookie):
Calories: 194 • Fat: 11g • Sodium: 121mg • Carbohydrates: 22g • Fiber: 1g • Sugar: 12g
Protein: 3g

Pink Lemonade Cookies

YIELDS
36
COOKIES

These pretty pink cookies are perfect for summer days. For even more lemon flavor, make this lemonade glaze: Start with 1 cup confectioners' sugar and add the thawed lemonade a tablespoon at a time, mixing until it reaches your preferred consistency. Spread on the completely cooled cookies. Place the sanding sugar on top of the glaze.

Recipe Prep Time: 10 minutes

Recipe Cook Time: 8 minutes

1 cup unsalted butter, softened
1 cup granulated sugar
2 large eggs
3 cups all-purpose flour
1 teaspoon baking soda
1 (12-ounce) can frozen pink lemonade, thawed and divided
A few drops red food coloring
2 tablespoons pink-colored sanding sugar

1. Preheat oven to 375°F. Line two baking sheets with parchment.

2. In a large bowl, use an electric mixer to cream butter and sugar until fluffy. Beat in eggs.

3. In a separate large bowl, combine flour and baking soda and then add to butter mixture. Add ¾ cup lemonade and a few drops of food coloring. Mix to combine.

4. Drop dough by rounded teaspoons onto prepared sheets.

5. Bake 8–10 minutes or until just barely brown. Brush tops of cookies with remaining lemonade and sprinkle with sanding sugar. Serve.

Per Serving (Serving size: 1 cookie):
Calories: 135 • Fat: 5g • Sodium: 40mg • Carbohydrates: 20g • Fiber: 0g • Sugar: 12g
Protein: 2g

Reese's Pieces Cookies

YIELDS **24** COOKIES

These irresistible cookies give a one-two punch of peanut butter by combining crunchy Reese's Pieces candies and creamy peanut butter chips. They are so delicious, they are guaranteed to disappear!

Recipe Prep Time: **10 minutes**

Recipe Cook Time: **8 minutes**

½ cup unsalted butter, softened
½ cup packed dark brown sugar
½ cup granulated sugar
1 large egg
1½ teaspoons vanilla extract
¼ teaspoon salt
½ teaspoon baking powder
½ teaspoon baking soda
1½ cups all-purpose flour
1 cup peanut butter chips
1 cup Reese's Pieces candies

1. Preheat oven to 350°F. Lightly grease two baking sheets or line with parchment.

2. In a large bowl, use an electric mixer on medium speed to cream butter, brown sugar, and granulated sugar. Add egg and vanilla. Mix completely.

3. In a separate large bowl, whisk together salt, baking powder, baking soda, and flour. Stir into butter mixture until blended.

4. Fold in peanut butter chips and Reese's Pieces. Drop dough by rounded teaspoons onto prepared sheets.

5. Bake 8–10 minutes or until just barely brown. Remove and cool. Serve.

Per Serving (Serving size: 1 cookie):
Calories: 191 • Fat: 9g • Sodium: 100mg • Carbohydrates: 25g • Fiber: 1g • Sugar: 17g
Protein: 4g

Ranger Cookies

YIELDS 30 COOKIES

Ranger Cookies are chock-full of delicious goodies, and they are so versatile. You can change the type of cereal, the type of chips, the type of nuts, or even leave one of them out altogether. For a sweet and salty twist, replace the cornflakes with coarsely crushed potato chips. Just remember to crumble the chips to about the size of cornflakes.

Recipe Prep Time: **10 minutes**

Recipe Cook Time: **10 minutes**

½ cup vegetable shortening
½ cup granulated sugar
½ cup packed light brown sugar
1 large egg
½ teaspoon vanilla extract
1 cup all-purpose flour
1 teaspoon baking soda
½ teaspoon baking powder
¼ teaspoon salt
1 cup cornflakes
1 cup quick-cooking oats
½ cup shredded sweetened coconut
½ cup butterscotch chips
½ cup chopped pecans

1. Preheat oven to 350°F. Lightly grease two baking sheets.

2. In a large bowl, use an electric mixer on medium speed to cream shortening, granulated sugar, and brown sugar until smooth. Beat in egg and vanilla.

3. In a separate large bowl, whisk together flour, baking soda, baking powder, and salt. Add to shortening mixture.

4. Fold in cornflakes, oats, coconut, butterscotch chips, and pecans. Drop dough by rounded tablespoons onto prepared sheets.

5. Bake 10–12 minutes or until golden brown with slightly soft middles. Cool and serve.

_____

Per Serving (Serving size: 1 cookie):
Calories: 117 • Fat: 5g • Sodium: 86mg • Carbohydrates: 16g • Fiber: 0g • Sugar: 10g
Protein: 1g

Triple Chocolate Frosted Cookies

YIELDS **24** COOKIES

Use good-quality chocolate in this recipe for best results. Mixing milk chocolate, dark chocolate, and bittersweet chocolate results in a more intense flavor and a deeper dimension to the final flavor. However, you can use just one kind of chocolate in the same total amount if you wish. Experiment until you find the chocolate taste that suits you the best.

Recipe Prep Time: **20 minutes**
Recipe Cook Time: **15 minutes**

Cookies
1 cup unsalted butter, softened
2 cups granulated sugar
3 large eggs
1½ tablespoons vanilla extract
2 teaspoons baking soda
5 cups all-purpose flour
½ teaspoon salt
1 teaspoon baking powder
2 cups whole buttermilk

Frosting
1 cup heavy cream
6 ounces milk chocolate, chopped
6 ounces dark chocolate, chopped
6 ounces bittersweet chocolate, chopped

1. Preheat oven to 350°F. Line two baking sheets with parchment.

2. To make Cookies: In a large bowl, use an electric mixer on medium speed to cream butter, sugar, and eggs until light and fluffy. Add vanilla.

3. In a separate large bowl, sift together baking soda, flour, salt, and baking powder. Whisk flour mixture into butter mixture alternately with buttermilk.

4. Drop dough by rounded tablespoons onto prepared baking sheets. Bake 15 minutes or until cookies spring back when lightly touched. Cool.

5. To make Frosting: Place cream in a medium saucepan over high heat and bring just to a boil. Remove from heat. Stir in milk, dark, and bittersweet chocolates until smooth and melted. Cool slightly. Mixture should be thick but spreadable.

6. Spread Frosting over tops of cooled Cookies in a thick ½" layer. Serve.

Per Serving (Serving size: 1 cookie):
Calories: 401 · Fat: 18g · Sodium: 218mg · Carbohydrates: 51g · Fiber: 2g · Sugar: 28g
Protein: 6g

White Chocolate Chip Macadamia

YIELDS
36
COOKIES

These rich cookies are crowd-pleasers. Using the pulp and seeds scraped from the inside of the vanilla bean gives these cookies a deep vanilla flavor. If you don't have a vanilla bean, it can be omitted.

Recipe Prep Time: 10 minutes, plus 30 minutes rest time

Recipe Cook Time: 8 minutes

1 cup unsalted butter, softened
1 cup packed light brown sugar
¾ cup granulated sugar
2 large eggs
2½ teaspoons vanilla extract
2 vanilla beans, split lengthwise
2¼ cups all-purpose flour
1 teaspoon baking soda
½ teaspoon salt
1 cup chopped macadamia nuts
1 cup white chocolate chips

1. Preheat oven to 350°F. Lightly grease two baking sheets.

2. In a large bowl, use an electric mixer to cream butter, brown sugar, and granulated sugar. Add eggs and vanilla extract. Scrape insides of vanilla beans into butter mixture. Set aside 30 minutes so flavors blend.

3. In a separate large bowl, stir together flour, baking soda, and salt. Blend into butter mixture.

4. Fold in macadamia nuts and white chocolate chips.

5. Drop dough by rounded teaspoons onto prepared sheets. Bake 8–10 minutes until golden brown. Cool on sheets 10 minutes before removing. Serve.

Per Serving (Serving size: 1 cookie):
Calories: 169 • Fat: 9g • Sodium: 78mg • Carbohydrates: 19g • Fiber: 1g • Sugar: 13g
Protein: 2g

M&M's Cookies

YIELDS 24 COOKIES

Using plain M&M's is the tradition for this recipe, but you can customize using any variety. For *Instagram*-worthy cookies, reserve about one-third of the M&M's from the dough and immediately press a few of them into the tops of the cookies when they come out of the oven.

Recipe Prep Time: **10 minutes**

Recipe Cook Time: **8 minutes**

½ cup unsalted butter, softened

½ cup packed dark brown sugar

½ cup granulated sugar

1 large egg

1¼ teaspoons vanilla extract

¼ teaspoon salt

½ teaspoon baking powder

½ teaspoon baking soda

1½ cups all-purpose flour

1 cup plain M&M's

1. Preheat oven to 350°F. Lightly grease two baking sheets.

2. In a large bowl, use an electric mixer to cream butter, brown sugar, and granulated sugar. Add egg and vanilla. Blend completely.

3. In a separate large bowl, whisk together salt, baking powder, baking soda, and flour. Stir into butter mixture until blended.

4. Stir in M&M's. Drop dough by rounded teaspoons onto prepared sheets.

5. Bake 8–10 minutes or until just barely brown. Remove and cool. Serve.

Per Serving (Serving size: 1 cookie):
Calories: 142 • Fat: 5g • Sodium: 70mg • Carbohydrates: 21g • Fiber: 0g • Sugar: 14g • Protein: 1g

CHAPTER 3
Brownies and Bars

Classic Blondies, Lemon Bars, Peanut Butter M&M's Bars—all your favorite bar cookie recipes are here. Layer on the flavor with Peanut Butter Crispy Brownie Bars, Raspberry Dreams, Homemade Twix Bars, and Key Lime Bars. The Mississippi Mud Brownies will delight chocolate lovers, and the Tiramisu Brownies are a deliciously easy twist on the Italian dessert. Once you see how easy it is to make brownies from scratch, you'll never settle for a box mix again.

Tiramisu Brownies

YIELDS
24
BROWNIES

This recipe uses finely grated chocolate as a final garnish to these rich Tiramisu Brownies. For a traditional finish, you can dust the tops of the brownies with sifted cocoa powder.

Recipe Prep Time: **15 minutes**

Recipe Cook Time: **35 minutes**

1 cup cake flour

¼ cup espresso powder

1 cup unsalted butter

12 ounces bittersweet chocolate

1⁷⁄₁₂ cups granulated sugar, divided

8 large eggs, divided

1 pound mascarpone cheese

2 teaspoons vanilla extract

¼ cup finely grated dark chocolate,
   for garnish

1. Preheat oven to 350°F. Lightly butter a 13″ × 9″ baking pan.

2. In a large bowl, combine flour and espresso powder and set aside.

3. In a medium microwave-safe bowl, melt butter and chocolate in microwave in 30-second increments, stirring in between until smooth. Cool slightly. Beat in 1⅓ cups sugar. Add 6 eggs, one at a time, beating well after each addition.

4. Fold in flour mixture. Pour batter into prepared pan, spreading evenly.

5. In a medium bowl, whisk together mascarpone cheese, remaining ¼ cup sugar, vanilla, and remaining 2 eggs. Pour mixture over brownie batter in pan. Bake 35–40 minutes or until top is set. Cool. Dust with grated chocolate and cut into bars. Serve.

Per Serving (Serving size: 1 brownie):
Calories: 312 • Fat: 19g • Sodium: 38mg • Carbohydrates: 29g • Fiber: 1g • Sugar: 21g
Protein: 5g

Rocky Road Brownies

YIELDS **12** BROWNIES

For extra chocolate flavor in these decadent Rocky Road Brownies, try adding 1 cup bittersweet chocolate chunks to the brownie batter. For the glaze, you can substitute the dark chocolate with bittersweet chocolate, Baker's German's sweet chocolate, semisweet chocolate, milk chocolate, or a combination of several types to get exactly the flavor you're craving!

Recipe Prep Time: 10 minutes

Recipe Cook Time: 27 minutes

Brownies
1 cup mini marshmallows
1 cup semisweet chocolate chips
½ cup chopped pecans
½ cup unsalted butter
1 cup granulated sugar
2 large eggs
1 teaspoon vanilla extract
½ cup unsweetened cocoa powder
½ teaspoon baking powder
⅛ teaspoon salt
½ cup all-purpose flour

Chocolate Glaze
6 ounces dark chocolate, chopped
3 tablespoons unsalted butter
1 tablespoon light corn syrup
½ teaspoon vanilla extract

1. Preheat oven to 350°F. Grease a 9″ square baking pan.

2. To make Brownies: In a medium bowl, stir together marshmallows, chocolate chips, and pecans. Set aside.

3. In a medium microwave-safe bowl, melt butter on high in microwave about 1 minute. Pour melted butter into a large bowl. Beat in sugar, eggs, and vanilla.

4. Add cocoa, baking powder, salt, and flour and blend well. Spoon batter into prepared pan and bake 20 minutes.

5. Open oven and sprinkle marshmallow mixture over top of Brownies. Close oven. Continue to bake until marshmallows have softened and puffed slightly. Remove from oven and cool.

6. To make Chocolate Glaze: Combine chocolate, butter, and corn syrup in a double boiler over low heat. Do not let water get above a simmer. Stir until ingredients melt and are smooth, about 5 minutes. Remove from heat. Add vanilla and blend well.

7. Drizzle warm Chocolate Glaze over top of Brownies. Cut into squares with a wet knife. Serve when cooled.

Per Serving (Serving size: 1 brownie):
Calories: 379 • Fat: 22g • Sodium: 67mg • Carbohydrates: 44g • Fiber: 4g • Sugar: 34g
Protein: 4g

Triple Layer Chocolate Peanut Butter Brownies

YIELDS
24
BROWNIES

Brownie, peanut butter, melted chocolate—each layer is more delicious than the last! Please remember: The base layer must be completely cool before you proceed with the next steps. You don't want the peanut butter layer to melt! Chill the brownies well before cutting to preserve all the layers. The finished brownies must be stored in an airtight container in the refrigerator.

Recipe Prep Time: 15 minutes, plus chill time between layers

Recipe Cook Time: 30 minutes

Base Layer
¾ cup unsalted butter
12 ounces bittersweet chocolate, chopped
1¼ cups granulated sugar
4 large eggs
2 teaspoons vanilla extract
½ teaspoon salt
1 cup all-purpose flour

Peanut Butter Layer
1 cup creamy peanut butter
¼ cup unsalted butter
¾ cup confectioners' sugar
⅛ teaspoon salt
1 tablespoon whole milk
1 teaspoon vanilla extract

Glaze
¼ cup unsalted butter
8 ounces bittersweet chocolate, chopped

1. Preheat oven to 350°F. Grease a 13″ × 9″ baking pan.

2. To make Base Layer: In a small microwave-safe bowl, melt butter and chocolate in microwave, stirring every 20 seconds. Transfer mixture to a large bowl.

3. Whisk in sugar until well blended and smooth. Beat in eggs one at a time, beating well after each. Add vanilla, salt, and flour. Mix until very well blended.

4. Spoon batter into prepared pan and bake 30–35 minutes or until a toothpick inserted into center comes out with just a few crumbs clinging to it. Cool completely before proceeding.

5. To make Peanut Butter Layer: In a large bowl with an electric mixer on medium speed, combine peanut butter and butter, mixing until smooth and creamy.

6. Stir in confectioners' sugar, salt, milk, and vanilla.

7. Spoon peanut butter mixture onto cooled brownie base. Chill.

8. To make Glaze: In a double boiler over low heat, melt butter and chocolate. Do not let water get hotter than a simmer. Mix until smooth.

9. Pour and smooth over chilled peanut butter layer. Cover brownies and chill for several hours before cutting. Serve.

Per Serving (Serving size: 1 brownie):
Calories: 363 • Fat: 22g • Sodium: 125mg • Carbohydrates: 34g • Fiber: 2g • Sugar: 26g
Protein: 5g

Raspberry White Chocolate Blondies

YIELDS
16
BLONDIES

If you're looking for a tangy, raspberry-forward flavor, you have to try these blondies! Dried raspberries have more flavor and contain less moisture than fresh berries, making them better for baking. For a variation, replace the raspberries with dried blueberries.

Recipe Prep Time: **10 minutes**
Recipe Cook Time: **35 minutes**

½ cup unsalted butter
12 ounces white chocolate chunks, divided
2 large eggs
½ cup granulated sugar
½ teaspoon almond extract
1 cup all-purpose flour
½ teaspoon salt
½ cup dried raspberries
½ cup chopped toasted almonds

1. Preheat oven to 325°F. Lightly grease and flour an 8″ square baking pan.

2. In a medium microwave-safe bowl, melt butter in microwave. Add half of white chocolate chunks. Stir well to combine.

3. In a separate medium bowl, beat eggs and sugar until well blended. Stir in butter mixture and almond extract.

4. Add flour and salt and stir until blended. Stir in dried raspberries, remaining white chocolate chunks, and almonds. Pour batter into prepared pan.

5. Bake 35 minutes or until bars are light golden brown and a knife inserted into center comes out clean. Do not overbake. Cool and serve.

Per Serving (Serving size: 1 blondie):
Calories: 258 • Fat: 14g • Sodium: 102mg • Carbohydrates: 29g • Fiber: 1g • Sugar: 22g
Protein: 4g

Classic Blondies

YIELDS 16 BLONDIES

These butterscotch-flavored brownies have been a favorite of kids and adults alike for decades. Use walnuts instead of pecans, or lose the nuts altogether! Sprinkle the tops of the blondies with some confectioners' sugar just before serving for a sweet touch.

Recipe Prep Time: 15 minutes

Recipe Cook Time: 30 minutes

2 cups all-purpose flour
1 teaspoon baking powder
1 teaspoon salt
¼ teaspoon baking soda
½ cup unsalted butter
1 cup packed light brown sugar
2 large eggs
1 teaspoon vanilla extract
1 cup chopped pecans
1 cup semisweet chocolate chips

1. Preheat oven to 325°F. Grease a 9″ square glass baking pan.

2. In a large bowl, sift together flour, baking powder, salt, and baking soda. Set aside.

3. In a medium microwave-safe bowl, melt butter and brown sugar in microwave, stirring until smooth. Transfer mixture to a large bowl and cool to room temperature.

4. Add eggs to butter mixture one at a time, beating well after each addition. Stir in vanilla.

5. Fold in flour mixture, pecans, and chocolate chips until well blended and no streaks of flour appear in the dough.

6. Spoon batter into prepared pan. Bake 30–35 minutes or until a toothpick inserted into center comes out with just a few crumbs clinging to it. Cool and cut into squares. Serve.

Per Serving (Serving size: 1 blondie):
Calories: 271 • Fat: 14g • Sodium: 210mg • Carbohydrates: 34g • Fiber: 2g • Sugar: 20g Protein: 4g

Espresso Brownies

YIELDS 36 BROWNIES

Calling all coffee lovers! These brownies are for those who absolutely jive with java. As a tip: Coffee beans are a great way to add flavor to any of your favorite brownie recipes. When freshly roasted, the beans are crunchy and can be used as a substitute for nuts, or you can grind or crush them to add a little coffee flavor.

Recipe Prep Time: **15 minutes, plus 8 hours chill time**

Recipe Cook Time: **40 minutes**

1¼ cups all-purpose flour
¼ teaspoon baking soda
⅛ teaspoon salt
1 cup granulated sugar
½ cup unsalted butter
¼ cup strong dark-roast coffee
¼ cup light corn syrup
12 ounces bittersweet chocolate, chopped
3 large eggs
2 teaspoons vanilla extract
8 ounces dark chocolate, chopped
½ cup coarsely chopped chocolate-covered
    coffee beans

1. Preheat oven to 325°F. Butter a 13″ × 9″ baking pan.

2. In a medium bowl, mix flour, baking soda, and salt and set aside.

3. In a medium microwave-safe bowl, combine sugar, butter, coffee, and corn syrup. Bring to a boil in microwave (about 5 minutes on high heat). Add bittersweet chocolate. Allow to stand without stirring for a few minutes. Transfer to a large bowl.

4. Beat chocolate mixture until smooth. Add eggs and vanilla and then flour mixture. Fold in dark chocolate and coffee beans.

5. Spoon batter into prepared pan. Bake 40–45 minutes or until a toothpick inserted into center comes out with just a few crumbs clinging to it.

6. Let brownies come to room temperature, then chill, covered, overnight. Cut into bars. Serve.

Per Serving (Serving size: 1 brownie):
Calories: 169 • Fat: 8g • Sodium: 28mg • Carbohydrates: 21g • Fiber: 1g • Sugar: 15g
Protein: 2g

Raspberry Dreams

YIELDS 16 BARS

You'll have to pinch yourself—these Raspberry Dreams seem too good to be real! This is a versatile bar that can be flavored several ways. Dried fruit purées or other jams and preserves can be substituted for the raspberry jam with equally delicious results.

Recipe Prep Time: **15 minutes**

Recipe Cook Time: **30 minutes**

1½ cups all-purpose flour
½ teaspoon salt
½ cup unsalted butter, softened
¾ cup granulated sugar, divided
2 large eggs, yolks and whites separated
1 cup seedless raspberry jam
1 teaspoon vanilla extract

1. Preheat oven to 350°F. Butter a 9" square baking pan.
2. In a large bowl, sift together flour and salt and set aside.
3. In a medium bowl, use an electric mixer on medium speed to cream butter and ¼ cup sugar until light and fluffy. Add egg yolks and beat until well blended.
4. Mix in flour mixture. Texture will be crumbly. Press dough firmly into baking pan. Spread jam evenly over top.
5. In a separate medium bowl, beat egg whites on medium speed until foamy. Gradually add remaining ½ cup sugar and beat on high speed until stiff, glossy peaks form. Blend in vanilla. Spread mixture over jam.
6. Bake 30 minutes until set. Cool completely before cutting into bars. Serve.

Per Serving (Serving size: 1 bar):
Calories: 194 • Fat: 6g • Sodium: 88mg • Carbohydrates: 32g • Fiber: 1g • Sugar: 19g
Protein: 2g

Chocolate Chip Brittle Cookies

YIELDS
48
COOKIES

These irregularly shaped bars are halfway between a cookie and a candy. Toasted nuts are essential to this recipe's complex flavor, but you can shake things up by using a different type of nut! To toast the nuts, spread them on a baking sheet in one layer and bake in a 375°F oven for 10 minutes or so. Watch them carefully so that they don't burn.

Recipe Prep Time: 10 minutes
Recipe Cook Time: 20 minutes

1 cup unsalted butter, softened
1 cup granulated sugar
2 teaspoons vanilla extract
2 cups all-purpose flour
1 teaspoon salt
1 cup toasted almonds
1½ cups chocolate chips, divided

1. Preheat oven to 375°F.

2. In a large bowl, use an electric mixer on medium speed to cream butter, sugar, and vanilla. Beat in flour and salt.

3. Stir in almonds and half of chocolate chips.

4. Press mixture gently into a 10″ × 15″ jelly roll pan. Bake 20–25 minutes or until golden brown. Cool.

5. In a medium microwave-safe bowl, melt remaining chocolate chips in microwave by microwaving on high heat in 30-second increments. Drizzle over cookies. Cool. Break cookie bars into irregular pieces. Serve.

Per Serving (Serving size: 1 cookie):
Calories: 166 • Fat: 7g • Sodium: 49mg • Carbohydrates: 13g • Fiber: 1g • Sugar: 8g
Protein: 1g

Mississippi Mud Brownies

YIELDS 24 BROWNIES

Marshmallow fans will love these rich and decadent brownies. You can substitute walnuts for the pecans and add 1 cup of coconut flakes to the frosting if you like.

Recipe Prep Time: **20 minutes**
Recipe Cook Time: **30 minutes**

1½ cups unsalted butter, divided

7 ounces unsweetened chocolate,
    chopped and divided

2 cups granulated sugar

4 large eggs

1 cup all-purpose flour

⅛ teaspoon salt

1 cup chopped pecans

½ cup evaporated milk

½ teaspoon vanilla extract

4½ cups confectioners' sugar

3 cups mini marshmallows

1. Preheat oven to 350°F. Grease a 13″ × 9″ baking pan.

2. In a small microwave-safe bowl, melt 1 cup butter in microwave. Stir in 4 ounces chocolate until melted. Cool. Move mixture to a large bowl.

3. Using an electric mixer on medium speed, beat sugar into chocolate mixture. Beat in eggs one at a time. Add flour and salt and blend until smooth. Fold in pecans.

4. Spread mixture in prepared pan. Bake 25–30 minutes or until a toothpick inserted into center comes out with only a few crumbs clinging to it.

5. In a medium saucepan over low heat, bring milk to a simmer. Add remaining ½ cup butter and remaining 3 ounces chocolate, stirring until chocolate is completely melted, about 5 minutes. Cool slightly. Add vanilla. Transfer mixture to a large mixing bowl and beat in confectioners' sugar until frosting is smooth but can still be poured.

6. Spread marshmallows evenly over top of warm brownies and quickly pour frosting over them. Cool and cut into bars. Serve.

Per Serving (Serving size: 1 brownie):
Calories: 377 • Fat: 19g • Sodium: 38mg • Carbohydrates: 47g • Fiber: 2g • Sugar: 38g
Protein: 4g

Lemon Bars

YIELDS **24** BARS

Looking for a sweet-and-sour classic? These Lemon Bars are sure to quench that thirst for citrus, and it's easy to substitute lemon with any other citrus flavor. Grapefruit, lime, orange, and tangerine all make delicious bars. If you are using a citrus fruit that is already sweet, like orange or tangerine, either use a little less sugar or reduce the amount of orange to ½ cup and add ¼ cup lemon juice.

Recipe Prep Time: **15 minutes**
Recipe Cook Time: **40 minutes**

Crust
1½ cups all-purpose flour
¼ teaspoon ground ginger
⅔ cup confectioners' sugar
¾ cup unsalted butter, softened

Topping
6 large eggs
1¾ cups granulated sugar
⅓ cup all-purpose flour
¾ cup fresh lemon juice
2 tablespoons grated lemon peel
2 tablespoons confectioners' sugar,
     for garnish

1. Preheat oven to 350°F. Lightly butter a 13" × 9" baking pan.

2. To make Crust: In a medium bowl, combine flour, ginger, and confectioners' sugar. Blend in butter with your fingers until mixture resembles coarse crumbs.

3. Press mixture into prepared pan. Bake 20 minutes or until golden brown.

4. To make Topping: In a large bowl, whisk together eggs, granulated sugar, flour, lemon juice, and lemon peel until foamy. Pour over hot Crust.

5. Return pan to oven and bake 20–25 minutes or until set. Cool completely.

6. Dust with confectioners' sugar, cut into bars, and serve.

Per Serving (Serving size: 1 bar):
Calories: 118 • Fat: 7g • Sodium: 18mg • Carbohydrates: 11g • Fiber: 0g • Sugar: 4g
Protein: 3g

Key Lime Bars

YIELDS **24** BARS

Not in the mood for a pie but still want the flavor? These Key Lime Bars will satisfy your craving in a snap. Key limes are small, tangy limes that grow in Key West, Florida, as well as in Mexico, California, and Central America. The juice is often available year-round in your local grocery store. The key lime juice in combination with delicate rose water results in a complex, refreshing note to this classic flavor profile!

Recipe Prep Time: **15 minutes**
Recipe Cook Time: **40 minutes**

Crust
1½ cups all-purpose flour
½ cup confectioners' sugar
¾ cup unsalted butter, softened
½ teaspoon vanilla extract
1 teaspoon rose water

Topping
4 large eggs
1½ cups granulated sugar
½ cup key lime juice
1 tablespoon all-purpose flour
1 tablespoon grated lime peel
2 tablespoons confectioners' sugar,
    for dusting

1. Preheat oven to 350°F. Butter a 13″ × 9″ baking pan.

2. To make Crust: In a large bowl, combine flour and confectioners' sugar. Add butter, vanilla, and rose water. Blend mixture with your fingers until it looks like coarse crumbs.

3. Gently but firmly press flour mixture into bottom of prepared pan. Bake 20 minutes or until golden brown.

4. To make Topping: In a large bowl, whisk together eggs, sugar, lime juice, flour, and lime peel. Blend well.

5. Pour mixture into Crust. Bake 20 minutes or until set. Cool. Dust with confectioners' sugar and cut into bars. Serve.

Per Serving (Serving size: 1 bar):
Calories: 152 · Fat: 6g · Sodium: 12mg · Carbohydrates: 22g · Fiber: 0g · Sugar: 15g
Protein: 2g

Homemade Twix Bars

YIELDS **16** BARS

Shortbread topped with caramel and rich chocolate; what's not to like? For a great variation, add 1 cup chopped pecans over the melted caramel layer before you add the ganache. When making ganache, use pure heavy cream. It is not the same as whipping cream, which is made of skim milk and chemicals.

Recipe Prep Time: **35 minutes**
Recipe Cook Time: **20 minutes**

Shortbread Layer
¾ cup unsalted butter
½ cup confectioners' sugar
1½ cups all-purpose flour

Caramel Topping
1 (14-ounce) bag caramels
⅓ cup evaporated milk
¼ cup unsalted butter

Ganache
1 cup heavy cream
1 cup chopped bittersweet chocolate
1 cup chopped milk chocolate
1 cup chopped dark chocolate

1. Preheat oven to 350°F. Lightly butter a 9″ square baking pan.

2. To make Shortbread Layer: In a medium bowl, combine butter, confectioners' sugar, and flour until blended and crumbly. Press dough into bottom of prepared pan. Bake 10–15 minutes until golden brown.

3. To make Caramel Topping: In a medium saucepan over medium-low heat, melt caramels, evaporated milk, and butter until smooth and blended, about 8–10 minutes. Spread over top of baked Shortbread Layer. Chill completely.

4. To make Ganache: In a medium microwave-safe bowl, heat cream in microwave until it almost comes to a boil, about 2 minutes. Remove, quickly add bittersweet, milk, and dark chocolate, and stir until smooth.

5. Allow mixture to cool slightly, then pour warm Ganache over Caramel Topping, using a flat spatula to smooth it out and evenly cover the entire surface.

6. Chill completely. Cut into bars and serve.

_____

Per Serving (Serving size: 1 bar):
Calories: 483 • Fat: 27g • Sodium: 86mg • Carbohydrates: 51g • Fiber: 2g • Sugar: 35g
Protein: 5g

Blueberry Crumble Bars

YIELDS
24
BARS

Blueberries are an antioxidant-rich superfood—they're great for your body and your taste buds! They're the star of the show in this recipe, but many different fruits can be substituted for the blueberries. Any seasonal fresh fruit will work well in these bars; just chop larger fruit like apples into small pieces.

Recipe Prep Time: **15 minutes**

Recipe Cook Time: **45 minutes**

1½ cups granulated sugar, divided

3 cups all-purpose flour

1 teaspoon baking powder

¼ teaspoon salt

Zest of 1 medium lemon

1 cup unsalted butter

1 large egg, beaten

1½ tablespoons cornstarch

4 cups blueberries

2 tablespoons lemon juice

1 cup white chocolate chips

1. Preheat oven to 375°F. Lightly grease a 13" × 9" baking pan.

2. In a medium bowl, combine 1 cup sugar, flour, baking powder, salt, and lemon zest. Using your fingers or a pastry cutter, cut in butter and beaten egg until mixture resembles coarse crumbs. Press half of crumb mixture into bottom of prepared pan.

3. In a large bowl, stir together cornstarch, remaining ½ cup sugar, blueberries, and lemon juice. Spoon blueberry mixture evenly over crust.

4. Sprinkle remaining crumb mixture on top of blueberry mixture. Bake 45–50 minutes until golden brown. Cool completely.

5. In a small microwave-safe bowl, melt white chocolate chips in microwave, stirring every 30 seconds until smooth. Drizzle over top. Cut into bars and serve.

Per Serving (Serving size: 1 bar):
Calories: 230 · Fat: 10g · Sodium: 55mg · Carbohydrates: 33g · Fiber: 1g · Sugar: 19g
Protein: 3g

Hawaiian Pineapple Bars

YIELDS **36** BARS

Embrace the tropics with these rich Hawaiian Pineapple Bars! Make sure the crushed pineapple is drained very well. Place in a colander and gently press out any remaining juice after draining; if it is too wet, the crust layer will be soggy. Store these bars in the refrigerator for up to 1 week.

Recipe Prep Time: **15 minutes**
Recipe Cook Time: **30 minutes**

Crust
2 cups all-purpose flour
1 cup granulated sugar
1 cup unsalted butter

Cream Layer
1 pound cream cheese, softened
⅓ cup granulated sugar
¼ cup heavy cream
2 teaspoons vanilla extract
2 cups crushed pineapple, drained

Topping
2 cups shredded coconut
1 tablespoon packed light brown sugar
3 tablespoons melted unsalted butter

1. Preheat oven to 350°F. Lightly butter bottom of a 13″ × 9″ baking pan.

2. To make Crust: In a medium bowl, mix flour and sugar. Blend in butter with fingers until mixture is crumbly. Pat dough firmly into bottom of prepared pan. Bake 15 minutes. Cool.

3. To make Cream Layer: In a separate medium bowl, use an electric mixer on medium speed to beat cream cheese, sugar, and cream. Add vanilla and blend well. Stir in pineapple and spread over Crust.

4. To make Topping: In a third medium bowl, mix coconut, brown sugar, and melted butter. Spread over Cream Layer.

5. Bake 15 minutes. Cool, then cut into bars. Serve.

Per Serving (Serving size: 1 bar):
Calories: 190 • Fat: 12g • Sodium: 61mg • Carbohydrates: 18g • Fiber: 1g • Sugar: 12g
Protein: 2g

Peanut Butter M&M's Bars

This recipe is as easy as it is delicious! If you really love peanut butter, use peanut butter M&M's instead of the plain chocolate variety.

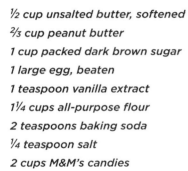

Recipe Prep Time: 10 minutes

Recipe Cook Time: 20 minutes

½ cup unsalted butter, softened

⅔ cup peanut butter

1 cup packed dark brown sugar

1 large egg, beaten

1 teaspoon vanilla extract

1¼ cups all-purpose flour

2 teaspoons baking soda

¼ teaspoon salt

2 cups M&M's candies

1. Preheat oven to 350°F. Grease a 13″ × 9″ baking pan.

2. In a large bowl, use an electric mixer on medium speed to cream butter, peanut butter, and brown sugar until smooth. Blend in egg and vanilla.

3. In a medium bowl, combine flour, baking soda, and salt. Gradually add to peanut butter mixture. Combine until crumbly.

4. Stir in M&M's. Press dough firmly into prepared pan.

5. Bake 20–25 minutes until set. Cool completely. Cut into bars and serve.

Per Serving (Serving size: 1 bar):
Calories: 223 • Fat: 11g • Sodium: 176mg • Carbohydrates: 28g • Fiber: 1g • Sugar: 21g
Protein: 3g

Peanut Butter Crispy Brownie Bars

YIELDS 36 BARS

Brownies, peanut butter, marshmallow, and crispy rice cereal all in one. These bars are sure to be a big hit at your house! The peanuts can be omitted if you prefer.

Recipe Prep Time: **15 minutes**
Recipe Cook Time: **15 minutes**

1⅓ cups all-purpose flour
½ teaspoon baking powder
¼ teaspoon salt
¼ cup cocoa
1 cup unsalted butter, softened
    and divided
1½ cups granulated sugar
3 large eggs
1 teaspoon vanilla extract
½ cup chopped peanuts
4 cups marshmallow crème
1 cup peanut butter
2 cups semisweet chocolate chips
2 cups crispy rice cereal

1. Preheat oven to 350°F. Lightly butter a 10″ × 15″ jelly roll pan.

2. In a large bowl, combine flour, baking powder, salt, and cocoa and set aside.

3. In a separate large bowl, use an electric mixer at medium speed to cream ¾ cup butter and sugar. Add eggs and vanilla and beat until fluffy. Add flour mixture and blend well. Fold in peanuts.

4. Spread batter in prepared pan and bake 15 minutes.

5. Using a knife dipped in hot water, spread marshmallow crème over top of brownies while they are still hot. Cool.

6. In a medium microwave-safe bowl, combine peanut butter, remaining ¼ cup butter, and chocolate. Melt in microwave on medium, stirring often until smooth and blended. Stir in rice cereal until combined. Spread mixture over bars and then chill. Serve.

Per Serving (Serving size: 1 bar):
Calories: 246 • Fat: 12g • Sodium: 69mg • Carbohydrates: 32g • Fiber: 1g • Sugar: 22g
Protein: 4g

CHAPTER 4
Shaped Cookies

While the shapes in this section are beautiful, don't be intimidated! They're easy and fun for the whole family. Most of the cookies in this chapter are shaped by hand by simply using your palms to roll lumps of dough into 1" or 2" balls before baking. Old-Fashioned Gingersnaps, Lemon Crinkles, Chocolate Snowballs, and Russian Chai Tea Cakes are all formed this way. Peanut Butter Cookies, Thumbprint Cookies, and Peanut Butter Blossoms require an additional step—simply flattening with a fork or your thumb or adding a piece of candy after the bake.

Thumbprint Cookies

YIELDS
36
COOKIES

Personalize these beautiful, yummy cookies with your thumb's indent! You may substitute almost any jam for the raspberry, and apricot, cherry preserves, or poppy seed filling all add a delicious sweetness. Pecans can be used in place of the walnuts.

Recipe Prep Time: **15 minutes**

Recipe Cook Time: **13 minutes**

1 cup unsalted butter, softened

½ cup packed light brown sugar

2 large egg yolks

½ teaspoon vanilla extract

½ teaspoon almond extract

2 cups all-purpose flour

¼ teaspoon salt

1¼ cups finely chopped walnuts

½ cup raspberry jam

1. Preheat oven to 350°F. Line two baking sheets with parchment.

2. In a large bowl, use an electric mixer on medium speed to beat butter and brown sugar until light and fluffy. Add egg yolks, vanilla, and almond extract.

3. In a medium bowl, combine flour and salt. Stir into butter mixture until well blended. Form dough into 1" balls and then roll balls in chopped walnuts until covered. Arrange balls on prepared sheets.

4. Bake 5 minutes. Carefully press your thumb down in the center of each cookie to create a dent and then fill the indentation with jam.

5. Bake 8–10 minutes more or until edges turn golden brown. Remove from oven and cool completely. Serve.

Per Serving (Serving size: 1 cookie):
Calories: 124 • Fat: 8g • Sodium: 19mg • Carbohydrates: 12g • Fiber: 1g • Sugar: 5g
Protein: 2g

Pecan Tassies

YIELDS
36
TARTS

Dainty pecan tarts are perfect for special occasions or holiday trays! Drizzle the tops with melted chocolate for a tasty garnish.

Recipe Prep Time: **15 minutes**
Recipe Cook Time: **15 minutes**

Tart Shells
1¼ cups unsalted butter, softened
8 ounces cream cheese, softened
2⅓ cups all-purpose flour

Filling
2 large eggs
1½ cups packed light brown sugar
2 tablespoons melted unsalted butter
½ teaspoon vanilla extract
⅛ teaspoon salt
1 cup chopped pecans

1. Preheat oven to 350°F. Lightly grease two mini muffin trays.

2. To make Tart Shells: In a large bowl, use an electric mixer on medium speed to beat butter and cream cheese until blended. Stir in flour until mixture forms a smooth, soft dough.

3. Roll into small 1" balls and push them into bottoms and slightly up the sides of mini muffin pan cups to form Tart Shells.

4. To make Filling: In a large bowl, blend eggs, brown sugar, butter, vanilla, and salt. Stir in pecans.

5. Add Filling to each Tart Shell, filling muffin cup about ⅔ full with nut mixture. Be careful not to overfill.

6. Bake 15–18 minutes or until Filling has puffed up and Tart Shells are golden brown. Cool and carefully remove tarts from pans. Serve.

Per Serving (Serving size: 1 tart):
Calories: 173 • Fat: 11g • Sodium: 38mg • Carbohydrates: 16g • Fiber: 1g • Sugar: 9g
Protein: 2g

Cinnamon Snaps

YIELDS
30
COOKIES

Who can say no to a simple cinnamon cookie? The dough needs to be chilled for at least 2 hours so it is easy to work with. Chill these cookies overnight for a better flavor and texture. While chilling, the gluten relaxes and will make your cookies more tender.

Recipe Prep Time: 15 minutes, plus 2 hours chill time

Recipe Cook Time: 20 minutes

¼ cup unsalted butter, softened

¼ cup vegetable shortening

1 cup granulated sugar

1 large egg

½ teaspoon vanilla extract

1⅓ cups all-purpose flour

½ teaspoon cream of tartar

½ teaspoon baking soda

¼ teaspoon salt

1 teaspoon ground cinnamon

¼ cup granulated sugar mixed with
    ½ tablespoon ground cinnamon,
    for rolling cookies

1. In a large bowl, use an electric mixer on medium speed to cream butter, shortening, and sugar until light and fluffy. Add egg and vanilla, beating thoroughly.

2. In a medium bowl, combine flour, cream of tartar, baking soda, salt, and cinnamon. Add to butter mixture and stir until well blended. Chill 2 hours.

3. Preheat oven to 350°F.

4. Place cinnamon sugar mixture on a small plate. Roll dough into small 1" balls. Roll each ball in cinnamon sugar mixture, then place about 2" apart on two ungreased baking sheets.

5. Bake 20 minutes. Remove from oven when cookies turn a dark golden brown. Cool and serve.

Per Serving (Serving size: 1 cookie):
Calories: 83 • Fat: 3g • Sodium: 43mg • Carbohydrates: 13g • Fiber: 0g • Sugar: 8g
Protein: 1g

Snickerdoodles

YIELDS
36
COOKIES

Snickerdoodles are a much-loved classic. These well-balanced, spiced cookies have a unique texture and taste, largely due to the cream of tartar used as part of the leavening.

Recipe Prep Time: **10 minutes, plus 30 minutes chill time**

Recipe Cook Time: **8 minutes**

1 cup unsalted butter, softened
1½ cups plus 2 tablespoons granulated sugar, divided
2 large eggs
2¾ cups all-purpose flour
1 teaspoon baking soda
2 teaspoons cream of tartar
⅛ teaspoon salt
2 teaspoons ground cinnamon

1. Preheat oven to 400°F. Line two baking sheets with parchment.

2. In a large bowl, use an electric mixer on medium speed to beat butter and 1½ cups sugar until smooth. Add eggs one at a time, beating well after each one.

3. In a large bowl, combine flour, baking soda, cream of tartar, and salt. Stir into butter mixture and blend well. Chill 30 minutes.

4. On a small plate, mix cinnamon and remaining 2 tablespoons sugar. Roll dough into walnut-sized balls. Roll each ball in cinnamon sugar mixture, then place 2″ apart on prepared sheets.

5. Bake 8 minutes. Cool and serve.

Per Serving (Serving size: 1 cookie):
Calories: 119 • Fat: 5g • Sodium: 47mg • Carbohydrates: 17g • Fiber: 0g • Sugar: 9g
Protein: 1g

Old-Fashioned Gingersnaps

YIELDS **36** COOKIES

Looking to get back to the basics? How about this spicy, crisp favorite? For a spicier cookie, add about ¼ teaspoon of cayenne pepper. It gives heat to the cinnamon without adding flavor. You'll find several different kinds of molasses at the grocery store. For most dessert baking, including this recipe, unsulfured molasses is the best choice. It has a milder flavor and less of an aftertaste than blackstrap molasses.

Recipe Prep Time: 10 minutes, plus 30 minutes chill time

Recipe Cook Time: 12 minutes

2 teaspoons baking soda

¼ teaspoon salt

2 cups all-purpose flour

1 teaspoon ground cinnamon

1 teaspoon ground ginger

¼ teaspoon ground cloves

¼ cup vegetable shortening

½ cup unsalted butter, softened

1¼ cups granulated sugar, divided

1 cup unsulfured molasses

1 large egg

1. In a large bowl, sift together baking soda, salt, flour, cinnamon, ginger, and cloves. Set aside.

2. In a separate large bowl, use an electric mixer on medium speed to cream shortening, butter, and 1 cup sugar. Blend in molasses and egg.

3. Add flour mixture to shortening mixture and blend well. Cover and chill a minimum of 30 minutes.

4. Preheat oven to 375°F. Lightly butter two baking sheets.

5. Place remaining ¼ cup sugar on a small plate. Roll dough into walnut-sized balls. Roll each ball in sugar, then place 2″ apart on prepared sheets. Bake 12 minutes. Cool completely and serve.

Per Serving (Serving size: 1 cookie):
Calories: 116 • Fat: 4g • Sodium: 92mg • Carbohydrates: 19g • Fiber: 0g • Sugar: 14g
Protein: 1g

Chocolate Snowballs

YIELDS **48** COOKIES

Chocolate Snowballs are crunchy, crumbly, chocolaty cookies that make a wonderful addition to a holiday assortment. These cookies must be cooled completely before they are rolled in the confectioners' sugar or else the sugar will melt off.

Recipe Prep Time: **10 minutes, plus 2 hours chill time**

Recipe Cook Time: **15 minutes**

1¼ cups unsalted butter, softened
⅔ cup granulated sugar
2 teaspoons vanilla extract
2 cups all-purpose flour
½ teaspoon salt
½ cup cocoa powder
½ cup confectioners' sugar

1. In a large bowl, use an electric mixer on medium speed to cream butter, sugar, and vanilla until creamy.

2. In a medium bowl, mix flour, salt, and cocoa. Blend into butter mixture. Chill a minimum of 2 hours.

3. Preheat oven to 350°F.

4. Roll dough into small 1" balls and place on two ungreased baking sheets. Bake 15 minutes.

5. Cool completely, then roll cookies in confectioners' sugar. Serve.

Per Serving (Serving size: 1 cookie):
Calories: 78 • Fat: 5g • Sodium: 25mg • Carbohydrates: 8g • Fiber: 0g • Sugar: 4g
Protein: 1g

Lemon Crinkles

YIELDS **48** COOKIES

Lemon Crinkles are a lemony cookie with the texture of a gingersnap or snickerdoodle. The secret to making perfect crinkle-topped cookies every time is to remove the cookies from the oven before they are completely done. As the cookies cool, the tops settle and create the cracks and crinkles that make these cookies just the right texture. The sugar melts slightly in the oven, giving the cookies a delicate crackly crust.

Recipe Prep Time: **15 minutes**

Recipe Cook Time: **10 minutes**

⅓ cup unsalted butter, softened

1¼ cups granulated sugar, divided

2 large eggs

3 tablespoons lemon juice

1½ teaspoons lemon extract

¼ teaspoon yellow gel food coloring

3½ cups all-purpose flour

2½ teaspoons baking powder

¼ teaspoon baking soda

1 teaspoon grated lemon peel

¼ teaspoon freshly grated nutmeg

½ teaspoon salt

1. Preheat oven to 375°F. Lightly grease two baking sheets.

2. In a large bowl, use an electric mixer on medium speed to cream butter and 1 cup sugar. Beat in eggs. Add lemon juice, lemon extract, and food coloring and combine.

3. In a separate large bowl, combine flour, baking powder, baking soda, lemon peel, nutmeg, and salt until well mixed. Stir into butter mixture, blending well.

4. Place remaining ¼ cup sugar on a small plate. Roll dough into walnut-sized balls. Roll each ball in sugar, then place 2″ apart on prepared sheets.

5. Bake 10 minutes. Remove from oven. Cool and serve.

Per Serving (Serving size: 1 cookie):
Calories: 68 • Fat: 1g • Sodium: 59mg • Carbohydrates: 12g • Fiber: 0g • Sugar: 5g
Protein: 1g

Rose Crackle Cookies

YIELDS
30
COOKIES

Want something a little more delicate for your taste buds? These sweet, subtle Rose Crackle Cookies are sure to impress. Rose water has a sweetly floral and very delicate flavor. You can easily find it online or at a specialty grocery store. The pink sanding sugar creates a lovely complement to the rose water.

Recipe Prep Time: 15 minutes, plus 2 hours chill time

Recipe Cook Time: 20 minutes

½ cup unsalted butter, softened

1 cup granulated sugar

1 large egg

¼ teaspoon vanilla extract

½ teaspoon rose water

1⅓ cups all-purpose flour

½ teaspoon cream of tartar

½ teaspoon baking soda

¼ teaspoon salt

3 tablespoons sanding sugar, with a few drops of rose water added

1. In a large bowl, use an electric mixer on medium speed to cream butter and sugar until light and fluffy. Add egg and beat well. Add vanilla and rose water and beat until smooth.

2. In a medium bowl, blend flour, cream of tartar, baking soda, and salt. Stir into butter mixture. Chill 2 hours.

3. Preheat oven to 350°F.

4. Place sanding sugar on a small plate. Roll dough into walnut-sized balls. Roll each ball in sugar, then place 2″ apart on ungreased baking sheets.

5. Bake 20 minutes. Cool completely and serve.

Per Serving (Serving size: 1 cookie):
Calories: 81 • Fat: 3g • Sodium: 43mg • Carbohydrates: 12g • Fiber: 0g • Sugar: 8g
Protein: 1g

Chai Chocolate Crackles

YIELDS
24
COOKIES

Savor all the sweetness of a spicy chai latte. Add a little chocolate, and you have the perfect cookie. The confectioners' sugar sets off the beautiful cracks that appear when the cookies bake. For a little heat, add ¼ teaspoon of cayenne when adding other spices.

Recipe Prep Time: 15 minutes, plus 30 minutes chill time

Recipe Cook Time: 18 minutes

¼ cup unsalted butter, softened

1 cup granulated sugar

2 large eggs

1 cup all-purpose flour

1 teaspoon baking powder

¼ teaspoon salt

½ teaspoon cardamom

¼ teaspoon cracked black pepper

5 tablespoons Hershey's Special Dark cocoa

⅛ cup confectioners' sugar

1. In a large bowl, use an electric mixer on medium speed to cream butter and sugar. Add eggs one at a time, beating well after each.

2. In a medium bowl, sift together flour, baking powder, salt, cardamom, pepper, and cocoa. Blend into butter mixture. Cover dough tightly and chill a minimum of 30 minutes.

3. Preheat oven to 300°F. Lightly grease two baking sheets.

4. Place confectioners' sugar on a small plate. Roll dough into tablespoon-sized balls. Roll each ball in sugar, coating thoroughly, then place 2″ apart on prepared sheets.

5. Bake 18–20 minutes or until cracks appear on the tops of cookies. Cool completely.

_____

Per Serving (Serving size: 1 cookie):
Calories: 78 • Fat: 2g • Sodium: 51mg • Carbohydrates: 14g • Fiber: 1g • Sugar: 9g
Protein: 1g

Peanut Butter Blossoms

YIELDS
48
COOKIES

This recipe calls for the original milk chocolate Hershey's Kisses to make these iconic cookies. But feel free to switch things up by using a different flavor of Kisses or replacing them with mini peanut butter cups. The turbinado sugar adds a nice crunch, but you can use granulated sugar if that's what you have on hand.

Recipe Prep Time: **15 minutes**

Recipe Cook Time: **8 minutes**

¼ cup vegetable shortening
¼ cup unsalted butter, softened
¾ cup peanut butter
⅓ cup granulated sugar
⅓ cup packed light brown sugar
1 large egg
2 tablespoons whole milk
1½ teaspoons vanilla extract
1½ cups all-purpose flour
1 teaspoon baking soda
½ teaspoon salt
⅓ cup turbinado sugar, for rolling
48 milk chocolate Hershey's Kisses,
     foil removed

1. Preheat oven to 350°F.

2. In a large bowl, use an electric mixer on medium speed to beat shortening, butter, and peanut butter until very well blended. Beat in granulated sugar, brown sugar, egg, milk, and vanilla until fluffy.

3. Add flour, baking soda, and salt and mix until well blended.

4. Place turbinado sugar on a small plate. Roll dough into 1" balls. Roll each ball in sugar, then place 2" apart on two or three ungreased baking sheets. Bake 8–10 minutes or until golden brown.

5. Remove from oven and immediately press a Kiss firmly in the center of each cookie. The sides will crack, but this is part of the charm of the cookie. Cool completely before serving.

Per Serving (Serving size: 1 cookie):
Calories: 99 • Fat: 5g • Sodium: 47mg • Carbohydrates: 11g • Fiber: 0g • Sugar: 7g
Protein: 2g

Everyone's Favorite Chocolate Sandwich Cookies

YIELDS **24** COOKIES

Ever wanted to try to make your own favorite packaged cookie, the Oreo? This recipe makes the traditional vanilla filling, but you can customize it to satisfy whatever flavor you're craving! To match that iconic flavor, use only Hershey's Special Dark cocoa for the outer cookie. Get creative with the flavor of the filling and come up with your own variations. Some suggestions are coffee, chocolate, peanut butter, mint, orange, or raspberry. These cookies *must* be stored in the refrigerator.

Recipe Prep Time: **20 minutes**

Recipe Cook Time: **18 minutes**

Cookies

1 cup Hershey's Special Dark cocoa, divided

1¼ cups granulated sugar, divided

¾ cup unsalted butter, softened

1 teaspoon salt

1 teaspoon espresso powder

1 large egg

1 tablespoon cold coffee

1 teaspoon vanilla extract

1½ cups all-purpose flour

Filling

1¼ teaspoons unflavored gelatin

2 tablespoons cold water

½ cup vegetable shortening

1 teaspoon vanilla extract

2½ cups confectioners' sugar

1. Preheat oven to 325°F. Line two baking sheets with parchment.

2. To make Cookies: In a medium bowl, place ¼ cup cocoa and ¼ cup sugar. Set aside.

3. In a large bowl, use an electric mixer on medium speed to beat remaining 1 cup sugar, butter, salt, and espresso powder until fluffy. Beat in egg, coffee, and vanilla. Stir in flour and remaining ¾ cup cocoa.

4. Roll dough into 2-teaspoon-sized balls. Place balls in bowl with sugar and cocoa mixture. Shake bowl until balls are thoroughly coated. Do this in batches if necessary.

5. Place balls on prepared sheets. Dip the bottom of a glass into the sugar-cocoa mixture and use it to press the balls flat. The Cookies should be about ⅛" thick.

6. Bake 18 minutes, being careful not to scorch. Cool completely.

7. To make Filling: In a small bowl, soften gelatin in water.

8. In a medium bowl, use an electric mixer on medium speed to beat shortening, vanilla, and confectioners' sugar until smooth. Add dissolved gelatin and beat until smooth.

9. Place a teaspoon of Filling between two cooled Cookies to make a sandwich. Serve.

Per Serving (Serving size: 1 cookie):
Calories: 211 • Fat: 10g • Sodium: 102mg • Carbohydrates: 29g • Fiber: 2g • Sugar: 21g
Protein: 2g

Russian Chai Tea Cakes

YIELDS
36
COOKIES

These tea cakes are delicate and crumbly cookies given a burst of flavor by spicy chai tea. Shape these cookies when they are icy cold. For the best results, only work with a third of the dough at a time, leaving the rest in the refrigerator until it is needed.

Recipe Prep Time: **10 minutes, plus 2 hours chill time**

Recipe Cook Time: **12 minutes**

1 cup walnuts

2 cups all-purpose flour, divided

2 teaspoons loose chai tea blend

1 cup unsalted butter, softened

1 teaspoon vanilla extract

½ cup plus 3 tablespoons confectioners' sugar, divided

1. Preheat oven to 350°F.

2. Place walnuts, 2 tablespoons flour, and chai in a blender. Pulse until walnuts are chopped finely but are not yet a paste.

3. In a large bowl, use an electric mixer on medium speed to cream butter and vanilla until well blended. Add ½ cup confectioners' sugar and remaining flour until blended. Fold in walnut mixture. Cover with plastic wrap and chill thoroughly at least 2 hours.

4. Measure dough into teaspoons and roll into balls. Place balls 2″ apart on two ungreased baking sheets. Bake 12 minutes. Cool.

5. Gently roll balls in remaining 3 tablespoons confectioners' sugar to coat. Cool and serve.

Per Serving (Serving size: 1 cookie):
Calories: 100 • Fat: 7g • Sodium: 0mg • Carbohydrates: 8g • Fiber: 0g • Sugar: 2g
Protein: 1g

Mexican Wedding Cakes

YIELDS
24
COOKIES

Craving a nutty, buttery cookie? Look no further. These Mexican Wedding Cakes must be shaped when they are icy cold. For the best results, only work with a third of the dough at a time, leaving the rest in the refrigerator until it is needed. Store cookies tightly covered for no more than 2–3 days.

Recipe Prep Time: **15 minutes, plus 1 hour chill time**

Recipe Cook Time: **18 minutes**

½ cup unsalted butter, softened
¾ cup confectioners' sugar, divided
1 teaspoon vanilla extract
1 cup all-purpose flour
½ cup pecans, toasted and ground
⅜ teaspoon ground cinnamon

1. In a large bowl, use an electric mixer on medium speed to beat butter until creamy. Add ¼ cup confectioners' sugar and vanilla and beat until mixture is well blended. Stir in flour and pecans. Cover with plastic wrap and chill thoroughly, at least 1 hour.

2. Preheat oven to 350°F. Line two baking sheets with parchment.

3. In a small bowl, mix cinnamon and remaining ½ cup confectioners' sugar. Set aside.

4. Break off dough in 2-teaspoon chunks, then form into crescents. Place on prepared baking sheets about 1″ apart. Bake 18–20 minutes or until bottoms are golden.

5. Cool on sheets about 5 minutes. Roll in cinnamon sugar mixture to coat completely. Cool and serve.

Per Serving (Serving size: 1 cookie):
Calories: 79 · Fat: 5g · Sodium: 0mg · Carbohydrates: 7g · Fiber: 0g · Sugar: 3g
Protein: 1g

Molasses Cookies

YIELDS
24
COOKIES

These large, chewy cookies are full of old-fashioned flavor. For best results, use Grandma's brand of unsulfured molasses. Rolling the balls of dough in turbinado sugar gives a nice crunch to the finished cookie, but you can use granulated sugar if you don't have turbinado sugar. If you love ginger, you can add ½ cup chopped candied ginger after all the ingredients have been thoroughly blended.

Recipe Prep Time: **10 minutes, plus 30 minutes chill time**

Recipe Cook Time: **10 minutes**

½ cup unsalted butter, softened
½ cup vegetable shortening
¾ cup unsulfured molasses
3 cups packed dark brown sugar
2 large eggs
3 cups all-purpose flour
½ teaspoon salt
1 tablespoon baking soda
1½ teaspoons ground cinnamon
1 teaspoon ground cloves
1½ teaspoons ground ginger
½ cup turbinado sugar, for rolling

1. In a large bowl, use an electric mixer on medium speed to beat butter and shortening until blended. Beat in molasses and brown sugar until creamy, and then beat in eggs one at a time.

2. In a separate large bowl, whisk together flour, salt, baking soda, cinnamon, cloves, and ginger. Add to butter mixture and blend thoroughly.

3. Chill, covered tightly, for 30 minutes.

4. Preheat oven to 350°F. Lightly grease two baking sheets.

5. Place turbinado sugar on a small plate. Using a tablespoon, measure out chilled dough and roll into balls. Roll balls in sugar.

6. Place balls on prepared sheets. Bake 10–12 minutes or until firm to touch. Cool completely and serve.

Per Serving (Serving size: 1 cookie):
Calories: 287 • Fat: 8g • Sodium: 224mg • Carbohydrates: 51g • Fiber: 1g • Sugar: 39g
Protein: 2g

Sausalito Cookies

YIELDS **40** COOKIES

These Sausalito Cookies have a little more flavor than a traditional chocolate chip cookie. They bake a bit longer than some other recipes to achieve a crispier texture. If you like them soft and chewy, take them out a minute or two sooner. If you like them thinner and flatter, use all butter rather than part shortening.

Recipe Prep Time: **10 minutes**

Recipe Cook Time: **15 minutes**

½ teaspoon baking powder

½ teaspoon salt

2½ cups all-purpose flour

½ cup unsalted butter, softened

½ cup butter-flavored shortening

¾ cup packed light brown sugar

¾ cup granulated sugar

1 large egg

1½ teaspoons vanilla extract

1 cup chopped macadamia nuts

12 ounces milk chocolate, chopped
    into large chunks

1. Preheat oven to 350°F. Lightly grease two baking sheets.

2. In a medium bowl, whisk together baking powder, salt, and flour.

3. In a large bowl, use an electric mixer on medium speed to beat butter and shortening until well blended. Beat in brown sugar and granulated sugar until fluffy. Add egg and vanilla.

4. Add flour mixture to butter mixture and blend well. Stir nuts and chocolate into dough.

5. Form dough into 1" balls and place on prepared sheets. Bake 15 minutes or until edges are golden brown. Cool and serve.

Per Serving (Serving size: 1 cookie):
Calories: 158 • Fat: 9g • Sodium: 45mg • Carbohydrates: 16g • Fiber: 1g • Sugar: 9g
Protein: 2g

Peanut Butter Cookies

YIELDS **46** COOKIES

Who can resist a classic peanut butter cookie? These cookies come together easily and have a perfectly sweet and buttery flavor. Make their iconic crisscross pattern by gently pressing the cookie dough with a fork before baking.

Recipe Prep Time: 10 minutes, plus 20 minutes chill time

Recipe Cook Time: 10 minutes

1 cup unsalted butter, softened

1 cup peanut butter

1 cup packed dark brown sugar

1 cup granulated sugar

2 large eggs

1 teaspoon vanilla extract

2½ cups all-purpose flour

1 teaspoon baking powder

½ teaspoon baking soda

½ teaspoon salt

1. Preheat oven to 375°F. Lightly grease two baking sheets or cover with parchment.

2. In a large bowl, use an electric mixer on medium speed to cream butter, peanut butter, brown sugar, and granulated sugar until fluffy. Add eggs and vanilla and mix until well combined.

3. In a separate large bowl, whisk together flour, baking powder, baking soda, and salt.

4. Gradually combine flour mixture with butter ingredients. Chill 20 minutes.

5. Roll dough into 1″ balls and place onto prepared sheets. Flatten balls with the back of a fork. Press each ball twice, making a crisscross pattern with the fork.

6. Bake 10 minutes or until golden brown. Cool and serve.

Per Serving (Serving size: 1 cookie):
Calories: 132 • Fat: 7g • Sodium: 78mg • Carbohydrates: 16g • Fiber: 0g • Sugar: 10g
Protein: 2g

CHAPTER 5

Rolled Cookies

Rolled cookies give the less-experienced, design-oriented baker the chance to shine! For rolled cookies, the dough is flattened using a rolling pin and then cut into shapes, usually with cookie cutters. A good-quality rolling pin makes the task easy and enjoyable. You can find cookie cutters in any shape online or in specialty baking or hobby stores. Or you can create a template of your desired shape out of parchment paper and cut around it with a sharp knife. If you are cutting dough into rectangles or diamonds, use a ruler to create straight, even lines and consistently sized cookies. To make the most of your dough, continue to recombine the excess after each cut and reroll it until you use up all the dough.

Sugar Cookies with Marble Glaze

YIELDS
40
COOKIES

These classic sugar cookies are soft, flavorful, and melt in your mouth. As a bonus, they can be cut into any shape. The glaze is as beautiful as it is simple to make. The marble effect is easy to create: Add drops of liquid food coloring to the glaze and swirl it around with a toothpick. Instead of spreading or pouring the glaze on the cookies, the cooled cookies are dipped in the glaze.

Recipe Prep Time: **30 minutes, plus 20 minutes chill time**

Recipe Cook Time: **8 minutes**

Cookies

1 cup unsalted butter, softened
1 cup granulated sugar
2 large eggs
2 teaspoons vanilla extract
1 teaspoon almond extract
2¾ cups all-purpose flour
¾ teaspoon baking powder
½ teaspoon salt

Glaze

4 cups confectioners' sugar
½ teaspoon vanilla extract
3 tablespoons whole milk
Liquid food coloring, as needed

1. To make Cookies: In a large bowl, use an electric mixer on medium speed to cream butter and sugar. Add eggs, vanilla, and almond extract. Mix completely.

2. Add flour, baking powder, and salt. Beat until combined. Divide the dough into two portions to make the rolling out process easier. Chill dough 20 minutes.

3. Preheat oven to 350°F. Lightly grease two baking sheets.

4. Roll dough out on a floured surface to about ½"–¼" thickness.

5. Use your favorite cookie cutter shapes to cut out the dough. Place Cookies about 1" apart on prepared baking sheets. Repeat until the dough is gone.

6. Bake 8 minutes or until golden brown. Cool completely.

7. To make Glaze: In a large bowl, combine confectioners' sugar and vanilla until blended. Add milk.

8. If you want to make a variety of colors, divide Glaze into separate bowls, one for each color. Add a few drops of food coloring to each bowl of Glaze. Swirl with a toothpick so ribbons of color appear. Move the toothpick in a zigzag pattern, removing and repositioning it at the end of each zigzag. Do not overmix. Distinct bands of color should remain; this is the marble effect.

9. Dip the top of each Cookie into Glaze and set aside to solidify. Serve.

Per Serving (Serving size: 1 cookie):
Calories: 142 • Fat: 5g • Sodium: 43mg • Carbohydrates: 22g • Fiber: 0g • Sugar: 15g
Protein: 1g

Scottish Shortbread

YIELDS
24
COOKIES

Sometimes simple is best—that's especially true in this recipe! Pair these classic buttery shortbread cookies with a cup of coffee or tea.

Recipe Prep Time: **15 minutes**

Recipe Cook Time: **20 minutes**

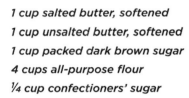

1 cup salted butter, softened

1 cup unsalted butter, softened

1 cup packed dark brown sugar

4 cups all-purpose flour

¼ cup confectioners' sugar

1. Preheat oven to 325°F. Place two baking sheets in freezer to chill.

2. In a large bowl, use an electric mixer on medium speed to cream salted butter, unsalted butter, and brown sugar. Mix in 3–3½ cups flour to make a soft dough. Add a little more flour if needed. Turn dough out onto a lightly floured surface and knead dough for a few minutes.

3. Roll dough out to ½" thickness on a surface covered with confectioners' sugar. Cut into rectangles. Place dough rectangles on chilled baking sheets.

4. Bake 20–25 minutes or until light golden. Cool completely and serve.

Per Serving (Serving size: 1 cookie):
Calories: 250 • Fat: 14g • Sodium: 64mg • Carbohydrates: 26g • Fiber: 1g • Sugar: 10g
Protein: 2g

Chocolate, Caramel, and Coconut Shortbread

YIELDS 30 COOKIES

Looking for a way to add some decadence to your favorite shortbread cookies? In this recipe, melt-in-your-mouth Scottish Shortbread is dipped in chocolate and then topped with caramel and coconut for an amazing taste. For best results, make the shortbread the day before you want to make these.

Recipe Prep Time: 10 minutes, plus 30 minutes chill time

Recipe Cook Time: 10 minutes

2 cups semisweet chocolate chips

30 Scottish Shortbread cookies, baked and cooled (see recipe in this chapter)

½ cup light corn syrup

½ cup granulated sugar

⅓ cup unsalted butter

½ cup sweetened condensed milk

½ teaspoon vanilla extract

4 cups coconut flakes, toasted

1. Line two baking sheets with parchment.

2. In a medium microwave-safe bowl, melt chocolate chips in the microwave by microwaving on high in 20-second increments. Stir every 20 seconds until chocolate is smooth.

3. Dip bottoms of shortbread cookies in chocolate. Place cookies on prepared sheets with chocolate side up. Put in refrigerator to harden for about 30 minutes.

4. Remove cookies from refrigerator. Turn them so chocolate side is down. In a medium saucepan over high heat, combine corn syrup, sugar, and butter. Bring mixture to a full boil, stirring constantly. Boil 3 minutes. Slowly add condensed milk, stirring constantly.

5. Reduce heat to low, and cook until mixture registers 220°F on a candy thermometer. Remove mixture from heat and stir in vanilla. Beat until creamy. Add coconut, stirring to blend well.

6. Working quickly, place a spoonful of coconut mixture on tops of cookies; gently press down with back of spoon. Cool completely. Serve.

Per Serving (Serving size: 1 cookie):
Calories: 423 • Fat: 23g • Sodium: 107mg • Carbohydrates: 50g • Fiber: 2g • Sugar: 31g
Protein: 4g

Rolled Sugar Cookies

YIELDS
36
COOKIES

These deliciously simple cookies are easy to roll and don't get tough if the dough is overworked, like some cookies. So, this is a great recipe for baking with kids! The actual yield of cookies in this recipe will vary depending on the size of the cookie cutters.

Recipe Prep Time: 10 minutes,
plus 8 hours chill time

Recipe Cook Time: 8 minutes

2 cups granulated sugar
1½ cups unsalted butter, melted
4 large eggs, beaten
1 tablespoon vanilla extract
5 cups all-purpose flour
1½ teaspoons baking powder

1. In a large bowl, whisk sugar into butter. Let mixture cool until lukewarm. Add eggs and vanilla and stir to combine. Stir in flour and baking powder.

2. Cover dough tightly and chill overnight.

3. Preheat oven to 375°F. Lightly grease two baking sheets.

4. Roll dough out to about ⅛" thickness on a lightly floured surface. Cut into desired shapes.

5. Bake 8–10 minutes or until cookies are light brown with golden edges. Cool and decorate as desired. Serve.

Per Serving (Serving size: 1 cookie):
Calories: 183 • Fat: 8g • Sodium: 29mg • Carbohydrates: 25g • Fiber: 0g • Sugar: 11g
Protein: 3g

Chocolate Rolled Cookies

YIELDS 36 COOKIES

Craving some chocolate? These cookies are worth the wait! Warning: This dough is quite soft and can be challenging to work with, so be sure to chill it overnight. If the dough is giving you trouble, try this trick: Roll chilled dough out between sheets of wax paper. Cut into shapes as desired, but leave the dough on the wax paper. Place the dough and wax paper in the freezer for several minutes to chill. Remove the chilled shapes and place them on the baking sheet with a spatula.

Recipe Prep Time: 10 minutes, plus 8 hours chill time

Recipe Cook Time: 8 minutes

3 ounces unsweetened chocolate

1 cup unsalted butter

1 cup granulated sugar

1 large egg

1 teaspoon vanilla extract

2 cups all-purpose flour

1 teaspoon baking soda

⅛ teaspoon salt

1. In a small microwave-safe bowl, melt chocolate and butter in microwave. Stir chocolate until it is blended and smooth. Move mixture to a large bowl. Blend in sugar until smooth. Blend in egg and vanilla.

2. In a medium bowl, whisk together flour, baking soda, and salt. Add to butter mixture, blending well. Cover dough tightly and chill overnight.

3. Preheat oven to 375°F. Line two baking sheets with parchment.

4. Roll dough out to about ⅛″ thickness on a lightly floured surface and cut into shapes.

5. Bake 8–10 minutes or until set. Cool completely. Decorate as desired and serve.

Per Serving (Serving size: 1 cookie):
Calories: 109 • Fat: 6g • Sodium: 46mg • Carbohydrates: 12g • Fiber: 1g • Sugar: 6g Protein: 1g

Animal Crackers

YIELDS 36 COOKIES

Sick of the bland animal crackers at the store? Try these delicious homemade ones! For the best flavor, use old-fashioned oats rather than quick or instant oats. Just be sure to grind the oats to a fine powder in a blender. Make certain that the blender is totally dry, or you will have paste.

Recipe Prep Time: **15 minutes**

Recipe Cook Time: **10 minutes**

½ cup old-fashioned oats

¼ teaspoon salt

¾ cup all-purpose flour

¼ teaspoon baking soda

¼ cup unsalted butter, softened

¼ cup buttermilk

2 teaspoons honey

¼ teaspoon maple extract

1. Preheat oven to 400°F.

2. Grind oats in blender until powdery, like flour. Transfer to a large bowl. Mix in salt, flour, and baking soda.

3. Using your fingers or a pastry cutter, cut in butter until mixture is like coarse crumbs. Add buttermilk, honey, and maple extract. Gather into a ball and knead lightly.

4. Roll dough out to about ⅛" thickness and cut with animal-shaped cookie cutters. Place shapes on two ungreased baking sheets.

5. Bake 10–12 minutes or until golden. Cool completely and serve.

Per Serving (Serving size: 1 cookie):
Calories: 27 • Fat: 1g • Sodium: 101mg • Carbohydrates: 3g • Fiber: 0g • Sugar: 0g Protein: 0g

Maple Sandwich Cookies

YIELDS
12
SANDWICH
COOKIES

An homage to a Canadian favorite, these may become your new go-to sandwich cookie! Maple leaf cookie cutters are available at many baking supply stores as well as online. The number of cookies you get from this recipe will depend on the size of the cutters you use. If you'd like more maple flavor, use maple sugar in place of the brown sugar in equal amounts.

Recipe Prep Time: **20 minutes, plus 8 hours chill time**

Recipe Cook Time: **8 minutes**

Cookies

1 cup unsalted butter, softened

1 cup granulated sugar

½ cup packed light brown sugar

2 large eggs

2 teaspoons vanilla extract

1 teaspoon maple extract

1 tablespoon pure maple syrup

3¼ cups all-purpose flour

½ teaspoon baking soda

½ teaspoon salt

Maple Filling

2 cups confectioners' sugar, divided

¼ cup vegetable shortening

1 large egg white

½ teaspoon vanilla extract

1 teaspoon maple extract

1. To make Cookies: In a large bowl, use an electric mixer on medium speed to cream butter, granulated sugar, and brown sugar until light and fluffy. Add eggs one at a time and beat well. Beat in vanilla, maple extract, and maple syrup.

2. In a large bowl, combine flour, baking soda, and salt. Stir into butter mixture. Cover dough and chill at least 8 hours or overnight.

3. Preheat oven to 375°F. Line two baking sheets with parchment.

4. Roll dough out to ⅛″ thickness on floured surface and then cut with cookie cutters. You'll need to cut out twenty-four leaves. If you don't have enough dough to make twenty-four, make sure you have an even number of Cookies. Place Cookies on prepared sheets.

5. Bake 8–10 minutes until light golden brown. Cool completely.

6. To make Maple Filling: In a large bowl, use an electric mixer on medium speed to combine ½ cup confectioners' sugar and shortening, beating until mixture is crumbly. Beat in egg white, vanilla, and maple extract. Add remaining 1½ cups confectioners' sugar and beat until smooth. You may need to thin the mixture with a little water. It should spread thickly but easily on Cookies.

7. Spread Filling on flat side of one Cookie. Add another Cookie to make a sandwich. Serve.

Per Serving (Serving size: 1 sandwich cookie):
Calories: 482 • Fat: 19g • Sodium: 171mg • Carbohydrates: 70g • Fiber: 1g • Sugar: 43g
Protein: 5g

Windmill Cookies

YIELDS
36
COOKIES

These thin and crispy cookies taste very similar to gingerbread. Traditionally, this dough is shaped in a windmill cookie mold. If you don't have a mold, you can use windmill-shaped cookie cutters.

Recipe Prep Time: **15 minutes, plus 8 hours chill time**

Recipe Cook Time: **15 minutes**

2 cups all-purpose flour
½ teaspoon baking powder
½ teaspoon salt
½ cup packed dark brown sugar
1 teaspoon ground cinnamon
½ teaspoon ground nutmeg
¼ teaspoon ground cloves
⅛ teaspoon ground cardamom
⅛ teaspoon ground ginger
1 cup unsalted butter
¼ cup whole milk
½ cup slivered almonds

1. In a large bowl, mix flour, baking powder, salt, brown sugar, cinnamon, nutmeg, cloves, cardamom, and ginger. Using your fingers or a pastry cutter, cut in butter and then add milk. Knead until a firm dough is formed. Cover and chill overnight.

2. Preheat oven to 350°F. Line two baking sheets with foil.

3. Roll dough out to ¼″ thickness on a floured surface. Cut with cookie mold or cookie cutters. Sprinkle tops of cookies with almonds.

4. Bake 15–20 minutes or until edges are golden. Cool and serve.

Per Serving (Serving size: 1 cookie):
Calories: 92 • Fat: 6g • Sodium: 41mg • Carbohydrates: 9g • Fiber: 0g • Sugar: 3g Protein: 1g

Lavender Diamonds

YIELDS 24 COOKIES

Lavender has an unusual flowery-citrus flavor that goes well with lemon or vanilla. Both are used here to give the cookies a complex yet mellow flavor. You can make a delicious lavender sugar by placing 1 tablespoon of food-grade lavender flowers and 2 cups of granulated sugar in a sealed cheesecloth bag and storing it for a day or so. The sugar will pick up the lavender flavor and is delicious as a garnish on top of cookies.

Recipe Prep Time: **15 minutes, plus 8 hours chill time**

Recipe Cook Time: **15 minutes**

1½ cups unsalted butter, softened

⅔ cup plus 2 tablespoons granulated sugar

¼ cup confectioners' sugar

1 tablespoon food-grade lavender flowers, chopped fine

1 teaspoon lemon zest

1 teaspoon vanilla extract

2½ cups all-purpose flour

½ cup cornstarch

¼ teaspoon salt

1. In a large bowl, use an electric mixer on medium speed to cream butter, ⅔ cup granulated sugar, and confectioners' sugar. Add lavender, lemon zest, and vanilla. Blend well.

2. In a medium bowl, whisk together flour, cornstarch, and salt. Blend into butter mixture. Cover and chill dough overnight.

3. Preheat oven to 325°F. Line two baking sheets with parchment.

4. Roll dough out to ¼" thickness on a floured surface. Cut into diamonds and place on baking sheets. Sprinkle tops of cookies with remaining 2 tablespoons granulated sugar.

5. Bake 15–20 minutes or until golden brown. Serve.

Per Serving (Serving size: 1 cookie):
Calories: 189 • Fat: 11g • Sodium: 26mg • Carbohydrates: 20g • Fiber: 0g • Sugar: 8g
Protein: 1g

CHAPTER 6
Slice and Bake Cookies

If you are a stickler for uniformity, you will love this chapter's slice and bake cookies. These cookies are cut from a log of chilled dough. To keep them perfectly round, set the log of dough upright in a drinking glass while it chills (or for the first hour if freezing). The dough lasts a long time—up to 1 month in the refrigerator or 12 months in the freezer. The great thing about slice and bakes is you can bake as many, or as few, as you want whenever you want. Keep a few rolls of a variety of doughs in your freezer, and you can quickly create a cookie assortment that will make it look like you have been baking for hours.

Chocolate Swirl Cookies

YIELDS
40
COOKIES

If you're looking to experiment with incorporating chocolate in a recipe, try this cookie! This recipe will work with any two colors of dough, though you must leave the chocolate out if you want brighter colors. Use food coloring to get the tints you want.

Recipe Prep Time: 10 minutes, plus 2 hours and 8 hours chill time

Recipe Cook Time: 10 minutes

½ cup unsalted butter, softened
½ cup granulated sugar
1 large egg yolk
1 teaspoon vanilla extract
3 tablespoons whole milk
1½ cups cake flour
½ teaspoon salt
1½ ounces bittersweet chocolate, melted

1. In a large bowl, use an electric mixer on medium speed to cream butter and sugar until fluffy. Beat in egg yolk, vanilla, and milk.

2. In a medium bowl, sift together flour and salt. Blend into butter mixture.

3. Divide dough into two halves. Add melted chocolate to one half of dough, mixing to incorporate. Chill dough 2 hours in the refrigerator.

4. Roll out each dough half into ⅛"-thick rectangles. Place one half on top of the other. Gently roll from one of the long ends so that the log has spirals of alternating doughs. Wrap tightly in wax paper and chill overnight or freeze.

5. When ready to bake, preheat oven to 375°F. Line two baking sheets with parchment.

6. Remove dough from wax paper and slice into ⅛"-thick slices. Place cookies on prepared sheets and bake 10–15 minutes until golden brown. Cool and serve.

Per Serving (Serving size: 1 cookie):
Calories: 56 · Fat: 3g · Sodium: 30mg · Carbohydrates: 7g · Fiber: 0g · Sugar: 3g
Protein: 1g

Date Pinwheels

YIELDS **33** COOKIES

Pinwheel cookies have a cute swirl pattern, which gives the cookies their name. If you like Fig Newtons, try making these with a fig filling rather than the date filling.

Recipe Prep Time: 20 minutes, plus 1–2 hours and 8 hours chill time

Recipe Cook Time: 13 minutes

Cookie Dough

¾ cup all-purpose flour

¼ teaspoon baking powder

¼ teaspoon baking soda

¹⁄₁₆ teaspoon salt

¼ cup unsalted butter, softened

¼ cup packed light brown sugar

¼ cup granulated sugar

1 large egg

¼ teaspoon vanilla extract

¼ tablespoon orange zest

Date Filling

6 tablespoons chopped dates

1¼ teaspoons granulated sugar

⅛ cup water

¼ tablespoon lemon juice

1. To make Cookie Dough: In a large bowl, sift together flour, baking powder, baking soda, and salt. Set aside.

2. In a separate large bowl, use an electric mixer on medium speed to cream butter, brown sugar, and granulated sugar until fluffy. Add egg, vanilla, and orange zest. Blend in flour mixture and chill 1–2 hours.

3. To make Date Filling: While dough is chilling, place dates, sugar, and water in a medium saucepan over medium heat. Stir often, until thickened, about 3–5 minutes. Take off heat and cool completely, then stir in lemon juice.

4. Remove dough from refrigerator. Roll dough into a 10" × 6" rectangle, about ⅛" thick. Spread with filling. Gently roll dough from one of the long ends so that the log has spirals of alternating dough and filling. Wrap dough log firmly in wax paper. Chill overnight or freeze.

5. When ready to bake, preheat oven 350°F.

6. Slice dough into ⅛"-thick slices. Place cookies 1" apart on two parchment-lined baking sheets. Bake 10–12 minutes or until cookies are set. Cool and serve.

Per Serving (Serving size: 1 cookie):
Calories: 42 • Fat: 1g • Sodium: 20mg • Carbohydrates: 7g • Fiber: 0g • Sugar: 4g Protein: 1g

Overnight Coconut Cookies

YIELDS **36** COOKIES

Looking to pay homage to the tropics? Try these sweet coconut-flavored cookies. Make them even prettier by rolling the logs of dough in finely chopped toasted coconut before chilling. Leave out the pecans if you're not a fan.

Recipe Prep Time: **10 minutes, plus 8 hours chill time**

Recipe Cook Time: **10 minutes**

6 tablespoons unsalted butter, softened

¾ cup packed light brown sugar

1 large egg

½ teaspoon vanilla extract

⅛ teaspoon salt

1 teaspoon baking powder

1½ cups cake flour

⅜ cup shredded coconut

¼ cup finely chopped pecans

1. In a large bowl, use an electric mixer at medium speed to cream butter and brown sugar until light and fluffy. Add egg and vanilla and blend well.

2. In a medium bowl, whisk together salt, baking powder, and flour. Stir into butter mixture. Fold in coconut and pecans.

3. Form dough into a 2½"-diameter log. Wrap in wax paper and chill in refrigerator overnight or freeze.

4. When ready to bake, preheat oven to 375°F. Line two baking sheets with parchment.

5. Slice dough into ⅛"-thick slices and place on prepared sheets. Bake 10 minutes or until just starting to brown. Cool and serve.

Per Serving (Serving size: 1 cookie):
Calories: 66 • Fat: 3g • Sodium: 27mg • Carbohydrates: 10g • Fiber: 0g • Sugar: 5g
Protein: 1g

Rainbow Butter Cookies

YIELDS
24
COOKIES

These beautiful, colorful cookies contain rainbow nonpareils to elevate a basic butter cookie recipe! You can customize this easy, versatile recipe by swapping out the nonpareils for other types of decorations. Try colored sanding sugar or any variety of sprinkles. Change up the flavor by rolling the log in mini chips or chopped nuts, or a mixture of both.

Recipe Prep Time: 10 minutes, plus 8 hours chill time

Recipe Cook Time: 8 minutes

½ cup unsalted butter, softened
½ cup granulated sugar
¾ teaspoon vanilla extract
1 large egg yolk
1¼ cups all-purpose flour
⅛ teaspoon salt
⅓ cup rainbow nonpareils

1. In a large bowl, use an electric mixer on medium speed to cream butter and sugar until fluffy. Add vanilla and egg yolk and beat until creamy.

2. In a separate large bowl, whisk together flour and salt. Mix into butter mixture.

3. Form dough into 2"-diameter logs. Wrap in wax paper and chill in refrigerator overnight or freeze.

4. When ready to bake, preheat oven to 350°F. Line two baking sheets with parchment. Place nonpareils on a medium plate.

5. Remove dough from wax paper and roll in nonpareils to cover all sides. Slice dough into ⅜"-thick slices and press the top sides into nonpareils again.

6. Place cookies 2" apart on prepared sheets. Bake 8–10 minutes until edges are golden in color. Cool and serve.

Per Serving (Serving size: 1 cookie):
Calories: 88 • Fat: 4g • Sodium: 13mg • Carbohydrates: 12g • Fiber: 0g • Sugar: 4g
Protein: 1g

Brown Sugar Cookies

YIELDS
36
COOKIES

A classic praline flavor makes these sugar cookies deliciously distinct. Add even more flavor by substituting vanilla butter and nut flavor extract for the vanilla.

Recipe Prep Time: 10 minutes, plus 2 hours chill time

Recipe Cook Time: 8 minutes

⅔ cup vegetable shortening

⅔ cup unsalted butter, softened

1 cup granulated sugar

1 cup packed dark brown sugar

2 large eggs

2 teaspoons vanilla extract

3¼ cups all-purpose flour

1 teaspoon baking soda

1 teaspoon salt

1 cup chopped pecans

1. In a large bowl, use an electric mixer on medium speed to mix shortening, butter, granulated sugar, and brown sugar until creamy and light. Add eggs one at a time, blending after each. Add vanilla and blend well.

2. In a medium bowl, sift together flour, baking soda, and salt. Add to butter mixture. Blend well and add pecans.

3. Form dough into a 1½"-diameter log. Wrap in wax paper and chill thoroughly in refrigerator at least 2 hours.

4. When ready to bake, preheat oven to 375°F.

5. Slice dough into ½"-thick slices and place on ungreased baking sheets. Bake 8–10 minutes or until set. Cool completely and serve.

Per Serving (Serving size: 1 cookie):
Calories: 175 • Fat: 9g • Sodium: 106mg • Carbohydrates: 21g • Fiber: 1g • Sugar: 12g
Protein: 2g

Cinnamon Crisps

YIELDS
24
COOKIES

These crispy cookies are perfect autumn treats! Add more cinnamon flavor with cinnamon-flavored chips, which are in the baking aisle next to the chocolate chips. Any nuts can be substituted for the almonds, or you can leave them out altogether.

Recipe Prep Time: 10 minutes, plus 8 hours chill time

Recipe Cook Time: 8 minutes

½ cup unsalted butter, softened
¾ cup granulated sugar, divided
1 large egg
1 cup all-purpose flour
2½ teaspoons ground cinnamon, divided
¼ teaspoon salt
½ cup toasted almonds

1. In a large bowl, use an electric mixer on medium speed to cream butter and ½ cup sugar until light and fluffy. Beat in egg.

2. Stir in flour, 1 teaspoon cinnamon, and salt. Blend well. Fold in almonds.

3. Form dough into a 2″-diameter log.

4. In a small bowl, combine remaining 1½ teaspoons cinnamon and ¼ cup sugar. Spread cinnamon sugar over a piece of wax paper. Roll dough log over sugar mixture, covering sides completely. Wrap log tightly in wax paper and chill overnight in refrigerator or freeze.

5. When ready to bake, preheat oven to 350°F. Lightly grease two baking sheets.

6. Slice dough into ¼″-thick slices and place 2″ apart on prepared sheets. Bake about 8 minutes or until golden. Cool and serve.

Per Serving (Serving size: 1 cookie):
Calories: 97 • Fat: 5g • Sodium: 27mg • Carbohydrates: 11g • Fiber: 1g • Sugar: 6g
Protein: 1g

Peanut Butter Whirligigs

YIELDS 30 COOKIES

Craving some childhood flavors? You can easily substitute your favorite flavor of jam for the chocolate in these peanut butter cookies. Be sure to use jam, as jelly does not work as well.

Recipe Prep Time: **10 minutes, plus 8 hours chill time**

Recipe Cook Time: **10 minutes**

½ cup vegetable shortening

½ cup peanut butter

½ cup packed light brown sugar

½ cup granulated sugar

1 large egg

1¼ cups all-purpose flour

½ teaspoon baking soda

½ teaspoon salt

6 ounces bittersweet chocolate, chopped and melted

1. In a large bowl, use an electric mixer on medium speed to cream shortening, peanut butter, brown sugar, and granulated sugar until light and fluffy. Beat in egg.

2. In a separate large bowl, whisk together flour, baking soda, and salt. Blend flour mixture into peanut butter mixture.

3. Roll dough into a ¼"-thick rectangle and spread melted chocolate over the top.

4. Gently roll from one of the long ends so that the log has spirals of alternating dough and chocolate. Wrap in wax paper and chill in refrigerator overnight or freeze.

5. When ready to bake, preheat oven to 375°F. Line two baking sheets with parchment.

6. Slice dough with a serrated knife into ¼"-thick slices and place on prepared sheets. Bake 10 minutes. Cool and serve.

Per Serving (Serving size: 1 cookie):
Calories: 135 • Fat: 7g • Sodium: 82mg • Carbohydrates: 15g • Fiber: 1g • Sugar: 10g Protein: 2g

Almond Butter Slices

YIELDS
24
COOKIES

These cookies have a subtle, light flavor. For a richer, sweet flavor, substitute ¼ cup light brown sugar for an equal amount of the granulated sugar.

Recipe Prep Time: 10 minutes, plus 8 hours chill time

Recipe Cook Time: 12 minutes

2 cups all-purpose flour
2 teaspoons baking powder
½ teaspoon baking soda
1¼ cups granulated sugar
1 cup unsalted butter
2 large eggs, divided
½ tablespoon almond extract
1 teaspoon water
24 whole almonds, for garnish
2 tablespoons granulated sugar,
    for sprinkling

1. In a large bowl, sift together flour, baking powder, baking soda, and granulated sugar. With your fingers or a pastry cutter, cut in butter until incorporated and the mixture looks like coarse crumbs. Add 1 egg and almond extract and mix well.

2. Form dough into a 1½"-diameter log. Wrap in wax paper and chill in refrigerator overnight or at least 8 hours.

3. When ready to bake, preheat oven to 350°F. Lightly grease two baking sheets.

4. Slice dough into ½"-thick slices and place on prepared sheets.

5. In a small bowl, mix remaining 1 egg with water to create an egg wash and brush on each cookie. Place an almond in center of each cookie. Sprinkle cookies evenly with sugar.

6. Bake 12–15 minutes. Make sure cookies do not brown. Cool completely and serve.

Per Serving (Serving size: 1 cookie):
Calories: 163 • Fat: 8g • Sodium: 74mg • Carbohydrates: 20g • Fiber: 0g • Sugar: 12g
Protein: 2g

Orange Pistachio Cookies

YIELDS
30
COOKIES

This recipe takes butter cookies to the next level by adding some orange and pistachio flavors! For more orange flavor, add ½ teaspoon of orange extract to the dough. Up the wow factor by dipping half of each baked cookie in chocolate glaze (white, milk, or dark) and sprinkling with extra chopped pistachios.

Recipe Prep Time: **10 minutes, plus 8 hours chill time**

Recipe Cook Time: **10 minutes**

½ cup granulated sugar
½ cup unsalted butter, softened
1 large egg
1 tablespoon orange juice
Grated zest of half a medium orange
1⅜ cups all-purpose flour
⅛ teaspoon baking soda
¼ cup finely chopped toasted pistachios

1. In a large bowl, use an electric mixer on medium speed to cream sugar and butter until fluffy. Beat in egg, orange juice, and orange zest.

2. In a medium bowl, whisk together flour and baking soda. Blend into butter mixture. Fold in pistachios.

3. Form dough into a 2"-diameter log. Wrap in wax paper and chill in refrigerator overnight or freeze.

4. When ready to bake, preheat oven to 375°F. Line two baking sheets with parchment.

5. Slice dough into ⅛"-thick slices and place 2" apart on prepared sheets. Bake 10 minutes or until golden brown. Cool and serve.

Per Serving (Serving size: 1 cookie):
Calories: 69 • Fat: 3g • Sodium: 8mg • Carbohydrates: 8g • Fiber: 0g • Sugar: 3g
Protein: 1g

Chocolate Thin Mint Cookies

YIELDS **36** COOKIES

If you are addicted to Girl Scout Thin Mints cookies, you will love these. Peppermint extract is available online and at most candy and cake supply stores. Don't mistake it for peppermint essential oil, which can be toxic in large doses!

Recipe Prep Time: 10 minutes, plus 8 hours chill time

Recipe Cook Time: 10 minutes

1 cup unsalted butter, softened
1 cup confectioners' sugar
1 teaspoon vanilla extract
1 cup cocoa powder
½ teaspoon salt
1½ cups all-purpose flour, sifted
12 ounces bittersweet chocolate chips
½ teaspoon pure peppermint extract

1. In a large bowl, use an electric mixer on medium speed to cream butter until light and fluffy. Add sugar and vanilla and blend well.

2. Mix in cocoa, salt, and flour.

3. Form dough into a 2"-diameter log. Wrap in wax paper and chill in refrigerator overnight.

4. When ready to bake, preheat oven to 350°F. Line two baking sheets with parchment.

5. Cut cookie dough as thin as possible without breaking. Place on prepared sheets and bake 10 minutes. Cool.

6. In a medium microwave-safe bowl, melt chocolate chips in microwave, stirring often. Add peppermint extract and stir to combine.

7. With a fork, dip cooled cookies completely in chocolate coating and gently tap off any excess. (If chocolate gets too thick to dip, reheat in microwave 15 seconds.) Place on clean parchment and use a toothpick to gently make swirls in chocolate. Let set and then serve.

Per Serving (Serving size: 1 cookie):
Calories: 132 • Fat: 8g • Sodium: 35mg • Carbohydrates: 14g • Fiber: 2g • Sugar: 7g
Protein: 2g

Chocolate Slice and Bakes

YIELDS
75
COOKIES

These cookies are perfect with a glass of cold milk! For a beautiful decoration, dip half of each cookie in white chocolate and top with chocolate sprinkles.

Recipe Prep Time: 10 minutes, plus 8 hours chill time

Recipe Cook Time: 10 minutes

9 tablespoons unsalted butter, softened
½ cup granulated sugar
1 large egg
1 tablespoon whole milk
1 teaspoon vanilla extract
1⅔ cups all-purpose flour
1½ teaspoons baking powder
¼ teaspoon salt
¼ cup cocoa powder

1. In a large bowl, use an electric mixer on medium speed to cream butter and sugar until fluffy. Add egg, milk, and vanilla and beat well.

2. In a medium bowl, whisk together flour, baking powder, salt, and cocoa. Blend into butter mixture.

3. Form dough into a 2″ diameter log. Wrap in wax paper and chill in refrigerator overnight or freeze.

4. When ready to bake, preheat oven to 350°F. Lightly grease two baking sheets.

5. Slice dough into ¼″-thick slices and place 2″ apart on prepared sheets. Bake 10–12 minutes or until tops of cookies are no longer shiny.

Per Serving (Serving size: 1 cookie):
Calories: 29 • Fat: 1g • Sodium: 18mg • Carbohydrates: 4g • Fiber: 0g • Sugar: 1g
Protein: 0g

Almond Roll

YIELDS **42** COOKIES

Looking for a light but flavorful cookie? Try these Almond Rolls! This recipe is delicious as is, or you can layer rectangles of dough, varying the color and/or flavor with each layer. The Chocolate Slice and Bakes (see recipe in this chapter) are a great recipe to combine with this one if you want to try this method. Make two (½"-thick) rectangles of each dough and alternate them. Wrap in wax paper and chill at least overnight. When you slice them, you will have rectangular striped cookies.

Recipe Prep Time: 10 minutes, plus 8 hours chill time

Recipe Cook Time: 10 minutes

6 tablespoons vegetable shortening
½ cup granulated sugar
1 large egg
½ teaspoon almond extract
1 cup all-purpose flour
⅛ teaspoon salt
¼ teaspoon baking soda
½ cup chopped blanched almonds

1. In a large bowl, use an electric mixer on medium speed to cream shortening and sugar. Beat in egg and almond extract.

2. In a medium bowl, whisk together flour, salt, and baking soda. Blend flour mixture into shortening mixture. Form dough into a 2"-diameter log and roll in chopped almonds.

3. Wrap dough roll in wax paper and chill in refrigerator overnight or freeze.

4. When ready to bake, preheat oven to 350°F. Lightly grease two baking sheets.

5. Slice dough into ⅛"-thick slices and arrange 2" apart on prepared sheets. Bake 10–12 minutes or until edges start to brown. Cool and serve.

Per Serving (Serving size: 1 cookie):
Calories: 48 • Fat: 3g • Sodium: 16mg • Carbohydrates: 5g • Fiber: 0g • Sugar: 2g
Protein: 1g

Checkerboard Slice and Bakes

YIELDS
30
COOKIES

Make your cookies fun by adding some color! Paste food coloring is essential to the coloring in this dough. Its thickness gives you much more control over the intensity and vibrancy of the color. Add the coloring to the dough a bit at a time, stirring thoroughly before adding more coloring. Continue this way, adding a little at a time, until you reach the color you want.

Recipe Prep Time: **15 minutes, plus 8 hours chill time**

Recipe Cook Time: **10 minutes**

½ cup vegetable shortening
1 cup granulated sugar
1 large egg
¾ teaspoons vanilla extract
¼ teaspoon almond extract
1¾ cups cake flour
½ teaspoon salt
1 teaspoon baking powder
Paste food coloring (two different colors)

1. In a large bowl, use an electric mixer on medium speed to cream shortening and sugar. Beat in egg, vanilla, and almond extract.

2. In a medium bowl, whisk together flour, salt, and baking powder. Blend flour mixture into shortening mixture.

3. Divide dough in half. Gradually add a different food coloring to each half until desired color is reached.

4. Working with color A, evenly divide the dough and make two ropes identical in diameter and length. Repeat with color B, matching the diameter and length of the color A ropes.

5. Lay one color A rope and one color B rope next to each other on a work surface. Lay one color B rope on top of one color A rope, and one color A rope on one color B rope. If you look at the dough stacks from the end, you should be able to see the checkerboard pattern.

6. Gently press ropes together and wrap in wax paper. Chill overnight.

7. When ready to bake, preheat oven to 375°F. Lightly grease two baking sheets.

8. Slice dough into ⅛"-thick slices and place 2" apart on prepared sheets. Cookies will be square rather than round.

9. Bake 10 minutes until cookies just start to turn brown. Cool and serve.

Per Serving (Serving size: 1 cookie):
Calories: 88 · Fat: 3g · Sodium: 57mg · Carbohydrates: 13g · Fiber: 0g · Sugar: 7g
Protein: 1g

Raisin Cookies

YIELDS **30** COOKIES

Sometimes shaking things up by adding some natural sweetness is exactly what a cookie needs. Try these Raisin Cookies for a fantastic alternative to chocolate chip. For a beautiful finish, sprinkle the tops with turbinado sugar just before baking. Gently press sugar into the cookie tops. It will form a crunchy crust as the cookies bake.

Recipe Prep Time: 10 minutes, plus 8 hours chill time

Recipe Cook Time: 8 minutes

¼ cup unsalted butter, softened

⅛ cup vegetable shortening

¾ cup packed light brown sugar

1 large egg

1½ cups all-purpose flour

¼ teaspoon salt

¼ teaspoon baking powder

¼ teaspoon ground nutmeg

¼ teaspoon baking soda

½ cup raisins

1. In a large bowl, use an electric mixer on medium speed to cream butter and shortening. Beat in brown sugar until fluffy. Add egg and beat well.

2. In a medium bowl, whisk flour, salt, baking powder, nutmeg, and baking soda. Blend into butter mixture. Fold in raisins. Form dough into a 2"-diameter log. Wrap in wax paper and chill in refrigerator overnight or freeze.

3. When ready to bake, preheat oven to 400°F. Lightly grease two baking sheets.

4. Slice dough into ⅛"-thick slices and place 2" apart on prepared sheets. Bake 8–10 minutes or until golden brown. Cool and serve.

_____

Per Serving (Serving size: 1 cookie):
Calories: 75 • Fat: 2g • Sodium: 38mg • Carbohydrates: 12g • Fiber: 0g • Sugar: 7g Protein: 1g

Lemon and Black Pepper Cookies

YIELDS 36 COOKIES

These are delightfully unusual cookies! Don't skip the overnight "marinade" of the dry ingredients. Mingling the ingredients greatly enhances flavor and is worth it. You can use either finely ground or coarsely ground black pepper—it depends on your preference—or try ground pink peppercorns for a more subtle flavor.

Recipe Prep Time: **10 minutes, plus 16 hours chill time, divided**

Recipe Cook Time: **8 minutes**

2 cups all-purpose flour

1 teaspoon baking powder

½ teaspoon baking soda

¾ teaspoon ground black pepper

¼ teaspoon salt

Grated zest of 1 medium lemon

½ cup unsalted butter, softened

1 cup granulated sugar

1 large egg

3 tablespoons whole milk

½ teaspoon vanilla extract

1 tablespoon lemon juice

1. In a medium bowl, whisk together flour, baking powder, baking soda, pepper, salt, and lemon zest. Place mixture in a zip-top bag. Seal and allow to stand overnight so lemon flavor permeates flour.

2. In a large bowl, use an electric mixer on medium speed to cream butter and sugar until light and fluffy. Add egg, milk, vanilla, and lemon juice and blend well. Stir in flour mixture and blend well.

3. Form dough into a 2"-diameter log. Wrap in wax paper and chill in refrigerator overnight or freeze.

4. When ready to bake, preheat oven to 350°F.

5. Slice dough into ¼"-thick slices and place on two baking sheets lined with parchment. Bake 8–10 minutes or until edges start to turn golden brown. Cool and serve.

Per Serving (Serving size: 1 cookie):
Calories: 72 • Fat: 3g • Sodium: 50mg • Carbohydrates: 11g • Fiber: 0g • Sugar: 6g
Protein: 1g

Cinnamon Roll Cookies

YIELDS 24 COOKIES

Enjoy the delicious taste of a cinnamon roll any time you want with these sweet cookies. This dough requires a 2-hour chill time during the preparation process in addition to the final overnight chill, so plan accordingly. Add ½ cup chopped pecans with the cinnamon and sugar mixture to add some additional texture and flavor.

Recipe Prep Time: 10 minutes, plus 2 hours and 8 hours chill time

Recipe Cook Time: 8 minutes

Cookies

1½ cups granulated sugar
½ cup vegetable shortening
½ cup unsalted butter, softened
2 large eggs
1½ teaspoons vanilla extract
1 cup whole milk
1 tablespoon cream of tartar
2 teaspoons baking soda
1 teaspoon salt
5 cups all-purpose flour
1 cup packed light brown sugar
2 tablespoons ground cinnamon

Glaze

2½ cups confectioners' sugar
⅓ cup light corn syrup
1 teaspoon vanilla extract
3–4 teaspoons warm water

1. In a large bowl, use an electric mixer on medium speed to cream granulated sugar, shortening, and butter until light and fluffy. Add eggs, vanilla, and milk and beat well.

2. In a medium bowl, whisk together cream of tartar, baking soda, salt, and flour. Beat into butter mixture. Cover dough and chill 2–3 hours.

3. In a small bowl, mix brown sugar and cinnamon.

4. Roll half of chilled dough into a rectangle on a piece of wax paper. Sprinkle half of sugar-cinnamon mixture over the top. Gently roll from one of the long ends so that the log has spirals of alternating dough and filling. Use wax paper to help roll. Wrap tightly in a clean sheet of wax paper and chill overnight. Repeat with remaining dough.

5. When ready to bake, preheat oven to 375°F. Line two baking sheets with parchment.

6. Slice dough into ⅛"-thick slices and place them 2" apart on sheets.

7. Bake 8–10 minutes or until done. Cool.

8. For the Glaze: In a large bowl with an electric mixer on medium speed, beat all ingredients except water until smooth.

9. Add water a few drops at a time until mixture is the desired consistency. Drizzle over cooled cookies and serve.

Per Serving (Serving size: 1 cookie):
Calories: 313 • Fat: 8g • Sodium: 213mg • Carbohydrates: 57g • Fiber: 1g • Sugar: 36g
Protein: 3g

Orange Date Pinwheels

YIELDS 30 COOKIES

These orange-flavored cookies with a sweet date filling are a vintage autumn treat. This dough requires a 2-hour chill time during the preparation process in addition to the final overnight chill, so plan accordingly. Tint the cookie dough orange for more fall fun. Enjoy with warm apple cider.

Recipe Prep Time: **25 minutes, plus 2 hours and 8 hours chill time**

Recipe Cook Time: **13 minutes**

Cookies

½ cup unsalted butter, softened
¼ cup granulated sugar
¼ cup packed light brown sugar
1 large egg
Grated rind of half a medium orange
1 tablespoon orange juice
½ teaspoon vanilla extract
½ teaspoon orange flavoring
2½ cups all-purpose flour
¼ teaspoon salt
⅛ teaspoon baking soda

Date Filling

¾ cup chopped dates
1 tablespoon plus 1 teaspoon granulated sugar
¼ cup water
½ tablespoon lemon juice

1. To make Cookies: In a large bowl, use an electric mixer on medium speed to cream butter, granulated sugar, and brown sugar until fluffy. Add egg, orange rind, orange juice, vanilla, and orange flavoring and beat well.

2. In a medium bowl, whisk together flour, salt, and baking soda. Blend into butter mixture. Chill dough 2 hours.

3. To make Date Filling: While dough is chilling, combine dates, sugar, and water in a small saucepan over medium heat and cook, stirring often, until thickened, about 3–5 minutes. Cool and stir in lemon juice.

4. Roll dough out into a rectangle and spread with Date Filling. Gently roll from one of the long ends so that the log has spirals of alternating dough and filling. Wrap in wax paper and chill in refrigerator overnight or freeze.

5. When ready to bake, preheat oven to 350°F. Line two baking sheets with parchment.

6. Slice dough into ⅓"-thick slices and place on prepared sheets. Bake 10 minutes or until golden. Cool and serve.

Per Serving (Serving size: 1 cookie):
Calories: 93 • Fat: 3g • Sodium: 28mg • Carbohydrates: 15g • Fiber: 1g • Sugar: 6g
Protein: 1g

Lemon Pistachio Swirls

YIELDS 30 COOKIES

These lemony cookies are light and refreshing with the richness of pistachios. For a delicious variation, replace the pistachios with poppy seeds and mix the filling in a bowl instead of a food processor. This dough requires a 2-hour chill time during the preparation process in addition to the final overnight chill, so plan accordingly.

Recipe Prep Time: **10 minutes, plus 2 hours and 8 hours chill time**

Recipe Cook Time: **10 minutes**

Cookies

½ cup unsalted butter, softened
⅓ cup confectioners' sugar
1 large egg yolk
¼ teaspoon vanilla extract
Grated zest of one medium lemon
¼ teaspoon salt
1 cup all-purpose flour

Pistachio Filling

¼ cup shelled pistachios
⅛ cup confectioners' sugar
1 large egg yolk
1 tablespoon water

1. To make Cookies: In a large bowl, use an electric mixer on medium speed to cream butter and sugar until light and fluffy. Add egg yolk and vanilla.

2. In a medium bowl, whisk together lemon zest, salt, and flour. Blend into butter mixture. Chill 2 hours.

3. To make Pistachio Filling: While dough is chilling, place pistachios and sugar in a food processor and process with on/off pulses until well ground. Add egg yolk and water and process to a smooth paste. Refrigerate until ready to use.

4. Roll dough out into a rectangle on a floured surface. Spread with pistachio mixture. Gently roll from one of the long ends so that the log has spirals of alternating dough and filling. Wrap tightly in wax paper. Chill overnight or freeze.

5. When ready to bake, preheat oven to 350°F. Line two baking sheets with parchment.

6. Slice dough into ¼"-thick slices and arrange on prepared sheets. Bake 10–12 minutes or until golden. Cool and serve.

Per Serving (Serving size: 1 cookie):
Calories: 57 • Fat: 4g • Sodium: 20mg • Carbohydrates: 5g • Fiber: 0g • Sugar: 2g
Protein: 1g

Neapolitan Cookies

YIELDS **44** COOKIES

You will need a loaf pan to make these pretty striped cookies. To change things up, the white dough can be altered by adding ¼ teaspoon coconut flavoring. Replace the pistachios with walnuts or pecans if you prefer.

Recipe Prep Time: **10 minutes, plus 8 hours chill time**

Recipe Cook Time: **10 minutes**

½ cup unsalted butter, softened
½ cup vegetable shortening
1½ cups granulated sugar
1 large egg
1 teaspoon vanilla extract
2½ cups all-purpose flour
1½ teaspoons baking powder
½ teaspoon salt
1 ounce unsweetened chocolate, melted
½ teaspoon almond extract
5 drops red food coloring
½ cup chopped pistachios

1. In a large bowl, use an electric mixer on medium speed to cream butter and shortening. Add sugar and beat until light and fluffy. Beat in egg and vanilla.

2. In a medium bowl, whisk together flour, baking powder, and salt. Blend into butter mixture.

3. Separate dough into three equal parts. Add chocolate to one part, almond extract and red food coloring to the second part, and pistachios to the third part. Mix each part thoroughly.

4. Line a 9″ loaf pan with wax paper. Spread pink portion of dough to cover bottom of pan. Spread nut portion over that and chocolate portion on top. Cover with wax paper and press down gently. Chill overnight.

5. When ready to bake, preheat oven to 350°F. Line two baking sheets with parchment.

6. Turn dough out of pan and slice lengthwise in ⅓″-thick crosswise slices. Place slices about 2″ apart on prepared sheets.

7. Bake 10–12 minutes or until edges are firm. Cool and serve.

Per Serving (Serving size: 1 cookie):
Calories: 105 • Fat: 5g • Sodium: 45mg • Carbohydrates: 13g • Fiber: 0g • Sugar: 7g
Protein: 1g

Strawberry Sandwich Cookies

YIELDS
30
SANDWICH
COOKIES

These cookies are very colorful and great for parties! Make them even prettier by rolling the dough log in sanding sugar or colored sprinkles before chilling. Change up the flavor by using a different type of gelatin, like orange, raspberry, cherry, or lemon. The finished cookies must be stored in an airtight container in the refrigerator because of the Cream Cheese Filling.

Recipe Prep Time: **20 minutes, plus 8 hours chill time**

Recipe Cook Time: **8 minutes**

Cookies

1½ cups unsalted butter, softened

1 cup granulated sugar

1 large egg

2 (4-serving size) packages strawberry gelatin, divided

1½ teaspoons vanilla extract

3½ cups all-purpose flour

1 teaspoon baking powder

Cream Cheese Filling

4 ounces full-fat cream cheese, softened

2 tablespoons plus 2 teaspoons unsalted butter, softened

1½ teaspoons vanilla extract

2 cups confectioners' sugar

1. To make Cookies: In a large bowl, use an electric mixer on medium speed to cream butter and sugar until light and fluffy. Add egg, 1½ packages gelatin, and vanilla. Blend well.

2. In a medium bowl, sift together flour and baking powder. Blend into butter mixture. Form dough into a 2"-diameter log. Wrap in wax paper and chill in refrigerator overnight.

3. Preheat oven to 400°F. Line two baking sheets with parchment.

4. Slice dough into ¼"-thick slices. You should get around sixty Cookies total—make sure it's an even number. Place Cookies on prepared sheets. Sprinkle half of Cookies with remaining ½ package of gelatin. Bake 8–10 minutes or until edges are firm. Cool completely. Keep the Cookies sprinkled with gelatin separate from the other half.

5. To make Cream Cheese Filling: In a large bowl, use an electric mixer on medium speed to mix cream cheese and butter until well blended. Beat in vanilla.

6. Slowly beat in confectioners' sugar until desired consistency is reached.

7. Spread about a tablespoon of filling on a Cookie not sprinkled with gelatin and top with a gelatin-sprinkled Cookie. Repeat with remaining Cookies. Serve.

Per Serving (Serving size: 1 cookie):
Calories: 234 • Fat: 11g • Sodium: 60mg • Carbohydrates: 30g • Fiber: 0g • Sugar: 18g
Protein: 2g

CHAPTER 7
Holiday Favorites

The holidays aren't complete without homemade cookies. From Gingerbread Men and Spritz Cookies to Cherry Snowballs and Lebkuchen, all the classics are here. Pumpkin Bars with Cream Cheese Frosting and Pecan Pie Bars make great desserts after your holiday meal. Indulge with Hot Buttered Rum Bars or Eggnog Cookies. Whether you're baking for friends and family, a cookie exchange, or yourself, you'll be feeling festive with these iconic recipes.

Gingerbread Men

YIELDS
36
COOKIES

This recipe makes a very soft dough, so be sure to keep it well chilled and allow plenty of room on the baking sheet for the dough to spread. For extra heat, replace the white pepper with cayenne pepper. If you would like these a bit more gingery, try increasing the ginger by ½ teaspoon. The yield will depend on the size of your cookie cutter.

Recipe Prep Time: 20 minutes, plus 8 hours chill time

Recipe Cook Time: 15 minutes

1 cup packed dark brown sugar

¾ cup granulated sugar

½ cup vegetable shortening

2 large eggs

¼ cup molasses

½ teaspoon vanilla extract

2¾ cups all-purpose flour

1 teaspoon baking soda

1½ teaspoons ground ginger

1 teaspoon salt

1 teaspoon ground cinnamon

¼ teaspoon white pepper

¼ teaspoon ground cloves

Royal Icing

2 tablespoons pasteurized egg whites

½ pound confectioners' sugar

½ tablespoon water

½ tablespoon lemon juice

Food coloring as desired

1. To make Cookies: In a large bowl, use an electric mixer on medium speed to cream brown sugar, granulated sugar, and shortening until fluffy. Add eggs, molasses, and vanilla.

2. In a medium bowl, whisk together flour, baking soda, ginger, salt, cinnamon, white pepper, and cloves until smooth. Add flour mixture to shortening mixture and blend well. Chill dough overnight.

3. Preheat oven to 300°F. Line two baking sheets with parchment.

4. Roll dough out to ⅛″ thickness on a heavily floured surface. Cut with floured cookie cutters and transfer Cookies to prepared sheets.

5. Bake 15–18 minutes or until edges are firm. Cool completely.

6. To make Royal Icing: In a large bowl, use an electric mixer to beat egg whites until foamy. Add confectioners' sugar and beat until mixture is smooth.

7. In a small bowl, mix water and lemon juice. Add to sugar mixture a few drops at a time until desired consistency is reached. Add food coloring as desired. Transfer icing to a piping bag and pipe onto cooled Cookies to decorate. Serve.

Per Serving (Serving size: 1 cookie):
Calories: 125 • Fat: 7g • Sodium: 37mg • Carbohydrates: 14g • Fiber: 1g • Sugar: 7g
Protein: 2g

Pumpkin Bars with Cream Cheese Frosting

YIELDS **40** BARS

These bars are a delicious addition to your Thanksgiving dessert table. They're also fantastic on any autumn day. Try adding ¼ cup of chopped candied ginger to the frosting for a sweet and spicy flavor. Frosted bars must be stored in the refrigerator and can be stored up to 1 week.

Recipe Prep Time: **20 minutes**

Recipe Cook Time: **30 minutes**

Bars

2 cups all-purpose flour

4 teaspoons baking powder

½ teaspoon salt

1 teaspoon ground cinnamon

1 teaspoon freshly grated nutmeg

1 teaspoon ground ginger

½ cup unsalted butter, softened

1 cup packed brown sugar

¼ cup granulated sugar

4 large eggs

1 pound mashed pure pumpkin

Cream Cheese Frosting

8 ounces full-fat cream cheese, softened

⅓ cup unsalted butter, softened

3 teaspoons vanilla extract

4 cups confectioners' sugar

1 tablespoon heavy cream, if needed

1. To make Bars: Preheat oven to 350°F. Butter a 10″ × 15″ jelly roll pan.

2. In a medium bowl, sift together flour, baking powder, salt, cinnamon, nutmeg, and ginger. Set aside.

3. In a large bowl, use an electric mixer on medium speed to cream butter, brown sugar, and granulated sugar until light and fluffy. Add eggs one at a time, beating well after each. Blend in pumpkin.

4. Stir flour mixture into butter mixture and blend well. Spread mixture evenly into prepared pan.

5. Bake 30–35 minutes or until top springs back when lightly touched. Cool completely.

6. To make Cream Cheese Frosting: In a large bowl, use an electric mixer on medium speed to mix cream cheese and butter until well blended. Beat in vanilla.

7. Slowly beat in confectioners' sugar until desired consistency is reached. If frosting is too thick when all of confectioners' sugar has been added, add cream to thin it out a little. Frost cooled Bars and serve.

Per Serving (Serving size: 1 bar):
Calories: 155 • Fat: 6g • Sodium: 108mg • Carbohydrates: 23g • Fiber: 1g • Sugar: 17g
Protein: 2g

Pecan Pie Bars

YIELDS
36
BARS

These bars taste just like pecan pie, but they are so much easier to make. You can also sprinkle 1 cup of chocolate chips over the crust before pouring on the filling for a chocolaty variation. Keep the finished bars in an airtight container in the refrigerator for up to 1 week.

Recipe Prep Time: **15 minutes**
Recipe Cook Time: **45 minutes**

Crust
3 cups all-purpose flour
½ cup granulated sugar
½ teaspoon salt
1 cup unsalted butter

Topping
1½ cups light corn syrup
4 large eggs
¾ cup granulated sugar
¾ cup packed light brown sugar
¼ cup unsalted butter, melted
1½ teaspoons vanilla extract
3 cups chopped pecans

1. Preheat oven to 350°F. Line a 10" × 15" jelly roll pan with parchment, allowing paper to slightly hang over sides and ends.

2. To make Crust: In a large bowl, stir together flour, sugar, and salt. With your fingers or a pastry cutter, cut in butter until mixture resembles coarse crumbs. Press firmly into prepared pan.

3. Bake 20 minutes.

4. To make Topping: In a medium bowl, mix corn syrup, eggs, granulated sugar, brown sugar, butter, and vanilla and whisk until smooth. Stir in pecans. Pour over hot Crust.

5. Bake 25 minutes or until set. Cool completely before cutting into bars. Serve.

Per Serving (Serving size: 1 bar):
Calories: 250 • Fat: 13g • Sodium: 51mg • Carbohydrates: 32g • Fiber: 1g • Sugar: 23g
Protein: 3g

Linzer Hearts

YIELDS 24 COOKIES

These delicate sandwich cookies are beautiful for Valentine's Day. If you don't have different-sized cookie cutters, use parchment paper to create a template for the smaller heart "window" and cut around it with a knife. Change up the recipe by using different cookie cutters and flavors of jam.

Recipe Prep Time: 20 minutes, plus 8 hours chill time

Recipe Cook Time: 12 minutes

¾ cup unsalted butter, softened

½ cup granulated sugar

½ teaspoon grated lemon rind

1 large egg

½ teaspoon vanilla extract

¼ teaspoon almond flavoring

1½ cups finely ground almonds

2¼ cups cake flour

½ teaspoon baking powder

½ teaspoon ground cinnamon

1 cup raspberry jam

⅛ cup confectioners' sugar, for dusting

1. In a large bowl, use an electric mixer on medium speed to cream butter. Add sugar, lemon rind, egg, vanilla, almond flavoring, and ground almonds. Beat until creamy.

2. In a medium bowl, whisk together flour, baking powder, and cinnamon. Blend into butter mixture to form a dough. Wrap dough tightly and chill overnight.

3. When ready to bake, preheat oven to 350°F. Line two baking sheets with parchment.

4. Roll dough out to ⅛" thickness on a lightly floured surface. Cut out forty-eight cookies with heart-shaped cookie cutters. In the center of twenty-four of the cookies, cut a smaller heart "window" using a cookie cutter or a knife and parchment paper template. Place cookies on prepared sheets and bake 12 minutes. Set aside.

5. In a medium microwave-safe bowl, heat jam in microwave for 30 seconds. Stir well. Spread a thin layer of jam on the tops of the twenty-four solid cookies. Don't overfill. Top each with a window cookie. Fill the windows with more jam, but don't overfill. Sprinkle with confectioners' sugar when cool. Serve.

Per Serving (Serving size: 1 cookie):
Calories: 190 • Fat: 8g • Sodium: 18mg • Carbohydrates: 25g • Fiber: 1g • Sugar: 11g Protein: 3g

Hot Buttered Rum Bars

YIELDS **24** BARS

These boozy treats are sure to make any gathering more festive. For a great variation on these bars, add 1 cup of pecans, walnuts, or macadamia nuts when you add the butterscotch chips to the batter before baking.

Recipe Prep Time: **10 minutes**

Recipe Cook Time: **25 minutes**

⅔ cup unsalted butter

½ cup granulated sugar

¼ cup packed light brown sugar

3 large eggs

¼ cup half-and-half

¼ cup rum

1½ cups all-purpose flour

1 teaspoon ground cinnamon

1 teaspoon ground ginger

½ teaspoon freshly grated nutmeg

¼ teaspoon ground cloves

¼ teaspoon salt

¼ cup butterscotch chips

1. Preheat oven to 350°F. Lightly grease a 9″ × 9″ square baking pan.

2. In a large bowl, use an electric mixer on medium speed to beat butter, granulated sugar, and brown sugar until light and creamy. Add eggs, half-and-half, and rum.

3. In a medium bowl, stir together flour, cinnamon, ginger, nutmeg, cloves, and salt. Blend into butter mixture.

4. Stir in butterscotch chips. Spread dough evenly in prepared pan.

5. Bake 25–30 minutes until a toothpick inserted into center comes out clean. Cool completely before cutting into bars. Serve.

Per Serving (Serving size: 1 bar):
Calories: 127 • Fat: 6g • Sodium: 37mg • Carbohydrates: 14g • Fiber: 0g • Sugar: 8g Protein: 2g

Peppermint Brownies

YIELDS
9
BROWNIES

These super-sized brownies go great with a mug of cocoa. Be sure to chill them thoroughly before cutting, or you won't get the layers. Use pure heavy cream, not whipping cream. Make them even more festive by coloring the peppermint layer pink with red food coloring. The finished brownies must be stored in an airtight container in the refrigerator.

Recipe Prep Time: **35 minutes, plus 4 hours chill time**

Recipe Cook Time: **25 minutes**

Base Layer

2 ounces unsweetened chocolate

½ cup unsalted butter

2 large eggs

1 cup granulated sugar

½ cup all-purpose flour

Middle Layer

1½ cups confectioners' sugar

3 tablespoons unsalted butter, softened

¼ cup heavy cream

½ teaspoon peppermint extract

¼ teaspoon vanilla extract

Top Layer

⅓ cup heavy cream

1½ cups semisweet chocolate chips

10 peppermint starlight mints, crushed

1. Preheat oven to 350°F. Grease and flour a 9″ square baking dish.

2. To make Base Layer: In a small saucepan over low heat, melt unsweetened chocolate with butter. Stir until smooth. Cool.

3. In a large bowl, use an electric mixer on medium speed to beat eggs and sugar. Blend in cooled chocolate and flour. Spread in prepared pan and bake 20–25 minutes or until a knife comes out clean. Cool completely.

4. To make Middle Layer: In a medium bowl, combine confectioners' sugar, softened butter, cream, peppermint extract, and vanilla. Beat until smooth. Spread on cooled brownies. Chill in refrigerator until firm.

5. To make Top Layer: In a small saucepan over low heat, bring cream to a simmer, about 5 minutes. Remove from heat. Add chocolate chips and stir until melted. Spread mixture quickly over peppermint layer. Sprinkle with crushed mints. Chill at least 4 hours. Cut into bars and serve.

Per Serving (Serving size: 1 brownie):
Calories: 613 • Fat: 33g • Sodium: 33mg • Carbohydrates: 76g • Fiber: 3g • Sugar: 63g
Protein: 5g

Spritz Cookies

YIELDS **36** COOKIES

Use a cookie press to make pretty shapes with this soft cookie dough. Spritz Cookies are delicate cookies that are beautiful when embellished. You can incorporate melted chocolate into this recipe if you like: Dip half of each cookie in chocolate, spread a layer of chocolate on the bottom of the cookie, or drizzle the cookie with chocolate stripes. Switch up the food coloring or omit it altogether and decorate with sprinkles or sanding sugar.

Recipe Prep Time: **15 minutes**
Recipe Cook Time: **12 minutes**

2¼ cups all-purpose flour
¼ teaspoon salt
¼ teaspoon ground cinnamon
1 cup unsalted butter, softened
3 ounces cream cheese, softened
1 cup granulated sugar
1 large egg yolk
1 teaspoon vanilla extract
½ teaspoon almond extract
Red paste food coloring
Green paste food coloring

1. Preheat oven to 350°F.

2. In a medium bowl, sift together flour, salt, and cinnamon.

3. In a large bowl, use an electric mixer on medium speed to blend butter and cream cheese. Beat in sugar until fluffy. Add egg yolk, vanilla, and almond extract.

4. Divide dough into three equal parts. Add red food coloring to one part, green food coloring to one part, and leave the last part as is.

5. Working with one color dough at a time, place dough in a cookie press or pastry bag with a decorative tip. Form cookies onto two ungreased baking sheets.

6. Bake 12–15 minutes until cookies are golden on the bottoms.

7. Cool completely and serve.

_____

Per Serving (Serving size: 1 cookie):
Calories: 105 • Fat: 6g • Sodium: 25mg • Carbohydrates: 12g • Fiber: 0g • Sugar: 6g
Protein: 1g

Eggnog Cookies

YIELDS
36
COOKIES

Even non-eggnog fans enjoy these festive cookies. For maximum flavor, purchase whole nutmegs and grate them yourself using a small grater. They are easy to grate and worth the effort. If you can't find rum extract, you can use brandy extract.

Recipe Prep Time: **15 minutes**
Recipe Cook Time: **6 minutes**

Cookies

¾ cup granulated sugar
¾ cup packed light brown sugar
¾ cup unsalted butter, softened
½ cup eggnog
1½ teaspoons vanilla extract
1 teaspoon rum extract
2 large egg yolks
1 teaspoon ground nutmeg
½ teaspoon ground cinnamon
2¼ cups all-purpose flour
1 teaspoon baking powder

Glaze

2½ cups confectioners' sugar
⅓ cup light corn syrup
1 teaspoon vanilla extract
3–4 teaspoons warm water

1. Preheat oven to 375°F. Line two baking sheets with parchment.

2. To make Cookies: In a large bowl, use an electric mixer on medium speed to beat granulated sugar, brown sugar, butter, eggnog, vanilla, rum extract, and egg yolks until light and fluffy.

3. In a medium bowl, combine nutmeg, cinnamon, flour, and baking powder. Blend into butter mixture until smooth.

4. Drop dough by rounded teaspoons onto prepared sheets. Bake 6–8 minutes or until just brown. Cool.

5. To make Glaze: In a medium bowl, use an electric mixer on medium speed to beat confectioners' sugar, corn syrup, and vanilla until smooth.

6. Add water a few drops at a time until Glaze is the desired consistency. Glaze each cooled Cookie and serve.

Per Serving (Serving size: 1 cookie):
Calories: 139 • Fat: 4g • Sodium: 19mg • Carbohydrates: 24g • Fiber: 0g • Sugar: 18g
Protein: 1g

Cranberry Pistachio Biscotti

YIELDS **36** COOKIES

Biscotti is first baked in loaves, then cut and baked again to achieve the crunchy texture everyone loves. The loaves are ready to cut when you can comfortably touch them and not get burned. Slice carefully on a diagonal in even slices and place the cookies flat on the baking sheet for the second baking. If you don't want to use the pistachios, you can substitute the same amount of toasted almonds.

Recipe Prep Time: **15 minutes**

Recipe Cook Time: **45 minutes**

¼ cup vegetable oil

¾ cup granulated sugar

2 large eggs

2 teaspoons vanilla extract

½ teaspoon almond extract

1¾ cups all-purpose flour

¼ teaspoon salt

1 teaspoon baking powder

¾ cup dried cranberries

1 cup unsalted pistachios

1. Preheat oven to 300°F. Line two baking sheets with parchment.

2. In a large bowl, use an electric mixer on medium speed to mix oil and sugar until blended. Add eggs, vanilla, and almond extract and combine.

3. In a medium bowl, combine flour, salt, and baking powder. Whisk flour mixture into oil mixture. Add cranberries and pistachios and stir to combine.

4. Divide dough in half. Form each half into a 12″ × 2″ rectangle and place on prepared sheets. Bake 35 minutes.

5. Remove from oven and cool 15 minutes.

6. Reduce oven to 275°F. Cut rectangles on the diagonal into ½″-thick slices. Lay cookies on sheets and return to oven.

7. Bake 10 minutes more. Cool completely. Serve.

Per Serving (Serving size: 1 cookie):
Calories: 83 • Fat: 3g • Sodium: 34mg • Carbohydrates: 12g • Fiber: 1g • Sugar: 6g
Protein: 2g

Cherry Snowballs

YIELDS 36 COOKIES

A creamy white exterior conceals the cheery, bright red inside of these cookies. These cookies would be perfect for Valentine's Day, Christmas, or whenever your sweet tooth needs a treat! Be sure to drain and dry the cherries very well before wrapping them in the dough, or the dough won't stay on the cherry.

Recipe Prep Time: **15 minutes**

Recipe Cook Time: **10 minutes**

36 maraschino cherries, drained, stemmed

1 cup unsalted butter, softened

½ cup confectioners' sugar

1 tablespoon water

2 teaspoons vanilla extract

½ teaspoon almond flavoring

½ teaspoon salt

2½ cups all-purpose flour

½ cup ground almonds

1 cup white chocolate pieces, melted

⅛ cup confectioners' sugar, for dusting

1. Preheat oven to 350°F.

2. Use paper towel to pat each cherry completely dry. Set aside.

3. In a large bowl, use an electric mixer on medium speed to cream butter, confectioners' sugar, water, vanilla, almond flavoring, and salt. Add flour and ground almonds and mix well.

4. Scoop a teaspoonful of dough and put a cherry in the middle. Wrap dough around cherry and set on an ungreased baking sheet.

5. Bake 10–15 minutes or until golden brown. Let cool.

6. Dip cookies halfway in melted white chocolate. Place chocolate side down on parchment paper to set. Dust snowballs with confectioners' sugar. Serve.

Per Serving (Serving size: 1 cookie):
Calories: 251 • Fat: 13g • Sodium: 75mg • Carbohydrates: 27g • Fiber: 1g • Sugar: 13g Protein: 3g

Chocolate Mint Checkerboards

YIELDS **48** COOKIES

Checkerboard cookies always look impressive, but the addition of a chocolate frame takes these cookies to the next level. They are sure to stand out on a Christmas cookie tray or as a sweet gift for someone special. You can use this frame technique on any type of checkerboard cookie.

Recipe Prep Time: 15 minutes, plus 8 hours chill time

Recipe Cook Time: 8 minutes

½ cup vegetable shortening
½ cup granulated sugar
1 large egg yolk
1½ teaspoons vanilla extract
1½ cups all-purpose flour
¼ teaspoon salt
½ teaspoon baking powder
3 tablespoons whole milk
1 ounce unsweetened chocolate, melted
Green paste food coloring
½ teaspoon peppermint extract, divided
Red paste food coloring

1. In a large bowl, use an electric mixer on medium speed to cream shortening and sugar until light and fluffy. Add egg yolk and vanilla and beat well.

2. In a medium bowl, sift together flour, salt, and baking powder. Blend flour mixture alternately with milk into shortening mixture.

3. Divide dough into three equal parts. Add chocolate to one part and mix thoroughly. Set aside.

4. Add green food coloring and ¼ teaspoon peppermint extract to a second part and mix thoroughly. Roll into two ropes, each ½" in diameter and the same length.

5. Add red food coloring and remaining ¼ teaspoon peppermint extract to remaining part and mix thoroughly. Roll into two ropes, each ½" in diameter and the same length.

6. On a piece of wax paper, place one green rope next to one red rope. Top the green rope with red and the red rope with green to create the checkerboard pattern. Press gently to attach the ropes to each other and create a log.

7. Roll out the chocolate dough and wrap it around the log. Press gently to help it attach. Wrap the log in wax paper. Chill in refrigerator overnight.

8. Preheat oven to 375°F. Lightly grease two baking sheets.

9. Slice dough thinly and arrange 2" apart on prepared sheets. Bake 8–10 minutes until set. Cool and serve.

Per Serving (Serving size: 1 cookie):
Calories: 47 • Fat: 2g • Sodium: 18mg • Carbohydrates: 5g • Fiber: 0g • Sugar: 2g
Protein: 1g

Lebkuchen

YIELDS **48** COOKIES

Everyone loves cookies fresh from the oven, but these cookies are actually best the next day. Store them in a closed container overnight to allow the flavors to develop. These spicy cookies are traditional German Christmas cookies that keep very well. Give each cookie plenty of space on the sheet when baking.

Recipe Prep Time: 20 minutes, plus 8 hours chill time

Recipe Cook Time: 12 minutes

Cookies

½ cup honey
⅛ cup molasses
½ tablespoon ground cinnamon
⅛ teaspoon freshly grated nutmeg
¾ teaspoon ground cloves
1 tablespoon chopped candied orange peel
1 tablespoon chopped candied citron
½ cup chopped blanched almonds
½ cup packed light brown sugar
¾ teaspoon orange zest
½ teaspoon lemon zest
¼ teaspoon baking soda
1 teaspoon hot coffee
1 large egg, beaten
2¼ cups all-purpose flour

Glaze

2½ cups confectioners' sugar
⅓ cup light corn syrup
1 teaspoon vanilla extract
3–4 teaspoons warm water

1. To make Cookies: In a large bowl, stir together honey, molasses, cinnamon, nutmeg, and cloves. Mix in candied orange peel, citron, almonds, brown sugar, orange zest, and lemon zest.

2. In a small bowl, stir baking soda into hot coffee. Beat coffee mixture into honey mixture. Beat in egg. Stir in flour. The dough will be very stiff, and you may need to knead the flour with your hands. Cover and chill overnight.

3. Preheat oven to 350°F. Line two baking sheets with parchment.

4. Roll dough out to ½" thickness on a floured surface. Cut into 2" × ¾" rectangles.

5. Place Cookies 2" apart on prepared sheets. Bake 12–15 minutes or until Cookies are just starting to brown. Cool.

6. To make Glaze: In a large bowl, use an electric mixer to beat confectioners' sugar, corn syrup, and vanilla until smooth.

7. Add water a few drops at a time until mixture is the desired consistency. Glaze each cooled Cookie. Store overnight and serve the next day.

Per Serving (Serving size: 1 cookie):
Calories: 84 • Fat: 1g • Sodium: 11mg • Carbohydrates: 18g • Fiber: 1g • Sugar: 13g
Protein: 1g

US / Metric Conversion Chart

VOLUME CONVERSIONS

US Volume Measure	Metric Equivalent
⅛ teaspoon	0.5 milliliter
¼ teaspoon	1 milliliter
½ teaspoon	2 milliliters
1 teaspoon	5 milliliters
½ tablespoon	7 milliliters
1 tablespoon (3 teaspoons)	15 milliliters
2 tablespoons (1 fluid ounce)	30 milliliters
¼ cup (4 tablespoons)	60 milliliters
⅓ cup	90 milliliters
½ cup (4 fluid ounces)	125 milliliters
⅔ cup	160 milliliters
¾ cup (6 fluid ounces)	180 milliliters
1 cup (16 tablespoons)	250 milliliters
1 pint (2 cups)	500 milliliters
1 quart (4 cups)	1 liter (about)

WEIGHT CONVERSIONS

US Weight Measure	Metric Equivalent
½ ounce	15 grams
1 ounce	30 grams
2 ounces	60 grams
3 ounces	85 grams
¼ pound (4 ounces)	115 grams
½ pound (8 ounces)	225 grams
¾ pound (12 ounces)	340 grams
1 pound (16 ounces)	454 grams

OVEN TEMPERATURE CONVERSIONS

Degrees Fahrenheit	Degrees Celsius
200 degrees F	95 degrees C
250 degrees F	120 degrees C
275 degrees F	135 degrees C
300 degrees F	150 degrees C
325 degrees F	160 degrees C
350 degrees F	180 degrees C
375 degrees F	190 degrees C
400 degrees F	205 degrees C
425 degrees F	220 degrees C
450 degrees F	230 degrees C

BAKING PAN SIZES

American	Metric
8 x 1½ inch round baking pan	20 x 4 cm cake tin
9 x 1½ inch round baking pan	23 x 3.5 cm cake tin
11 x 7 x 1½ inch baking pan	28 x 18 x 4 cm baking tin
13 x 9 x 2 inch baking pan	30 x 20 x 5 cm baking tin
2 quart rectangular baking dish	30 x 20 x 3 cm baking tin
15 x 10 x 2 inch baking pan	30 x 25 x 2 cm baking tin (Swiss roll tin)
9 inch pie plate	22 x 4 or 23 x 4 cm pie plate
7 or 8 inch springform pan	18 or 20 cm springform or loose bottom cake tin
9 x 5 x 3 inch loaf pan	23 x 13 x 7 cm or 2 lb narrow loaf or pate tin
1½ quart casserole	1.5 liter casserole
2 quart casserole	2 liter casserole

Index

c

D